Christine Schirr

Islam and Democracy

WEA
World Evangelical Alliance

IIIS
International Institute
of Islamic Studies

International Institute for Religious Freedom
IIRF

The WEA Global Issues Series

Editors:

Bishop Efraim Tendero, Philippines

Secretary General, World Evangelical Alliance

Thomas Schirrmacher

Director, International Institute for Religious Freedom,
Associate Secretary General for Theological Concerns, World Evangelical Alliance

Volumes:

"The WEA Global Issues Series is designed to provide thoughtful, practical, and biblical insights from an Evangelical Christian perspective into some of the greatest challenges we face in the world. I trust you will find this volume enriching and helpful in your life and Kingdom service."

Christine Schirrmacher

Islam and Democracy:

Can They Be Reconciled?

Translated by Richard McClary
Edited with a foreword by Thomas K. Johnson
Assisted by Ruth Baldwin

WIPF & STOCK · Eugene, Oregon

Wipf and Stock Publishers
199 W 8th Ave, Suite 3
Eugene, OR 97401

Islam and Democracy
Can They Be Reconciled?
By Schirrmacher, Christine
Copyright © 2020 Verlag für Kultur und Wissenschaft Culture and Science Publ.
All rights reserved.
Softcover ISBN-13: 978-1-7252-9440-0
Hardcover ISBN-13: 978-1-7252-9439-4
Publication date 12/4/2020
Previously published by Verlag für Kultur und Wissenschaft Culture and Science Publ., 2020

Contents

Foreword

Sometimes a question we have long considered suddenly becomes urgent. During the week when I first read Prof. Schirrmacher's essay on Islam and democracy, the news reports in Europe were filled with stories, many with horrible endings, of refugees fleeing from Iraq and Syria, hoping to find safety and a future within Europe. Another stream of refugees is flowing from South Yemen. Most are fleeing the brutal civil wars in their homelands, wars that are killing people by the hundreds of thousands while also devastating their homes, businesses, agriculture, and schools. Despair must fill their minds after witnessing death and destruction, leading them to take terrible risks to cross the Mediterranean and Aegean seas, often at the hands of human traffickers on boats prone to sink or capsize. The pictures of their corpses floating on the waves should be only a matter of nightmares, not the reality it is. I am reminded of the sage words of Thomas Hobbes, that the condition of humanity in the state of the war of all against all is "solitary, poor, nasty, brutish, and short."[1]

Most of the war refugees are coming from the lands we usually describe as "Muslim majority" countries. This way of speaking has the advantage of reminding us that there are religious minorities in almost every country on earth, and some such minorities are large. And one must never forget that Islam itself is rather diverse, with numerous local varieties, in addition to the well-known major traditions within Islam. Obviously the strange ideology of the "Islamic State," one of the versions of the new radical Islam, is the cause of much of the current fighting, an ideology that millions of Muslims would reject. Thus the urgent question, how easy is it for peaceful democracies to arise within Muslim majority countries?

We must not exaggerate the extent to which democracies are peaceful. I have heard democracy described as a continuous non-violent civil war. And I am bothered by the extent to which our discourse within western democracies often falls outside the bounds of what I would describe as "civil discourse," being filled with hostility and militancy, even hatred at times. But we must not underestimate the value of the fact that our deepest political disagreements within democracies are usually fought with words in courts, parliaments, and news reports, not with bullets and

---

[1]   This famous quotation is found in Thomas Hobbes, *Leviathan*, 1651. Hobbes was familiar with the death and destruction caused by both the Thirty Years' War (1618-1648) in continental Europe and by the English Civil War (1642-1651).

bombs. After a battle of words in a democracy, people usually go home or to a restaurant to eat and drink, not going first to a cemetery, or worse, leaving the bodies of their friends and relatives in the rubble of their homes. This difference is simply huge.

Relatively peaceful democracies do not grow out of thin air. There is always a cultural heritage, the software of the human heart and mind, that shapes the way in which people create and develop public institutions, whether government, business, health care, or education. I agree with those analysts who say that healthy visible public institutions are always dependent on health in the invisible realm of culture. And religions always play an important role, sometimes a predominant role, in the culture and heritage of a people. Can healthy democracies arise within a cultural context that is heavily influenced by Islam? If one happens to be in the territories controlled by ISIS, the answer is clearly "NO!" But if one happens to be in Indonesia, the answer seems to be "yes." There is certainly much to discuss.

Not only do the varieties within Islam matter with regard to our question. There are different types of democracies and different definitions of democracy. French democracy is different from German democracy, with Prof. Schirrmacher representing a very reputable German model of democracy. However, one must be careful about calling a country a democracy simply because a journalist or two has used that word, or even if an election has been held. At the very least, I would want to see a system of judges and courts that is independent from the executive branch of government, along with protection of basic human rights, including freedom of religion, before I would want to apply the label "democracy." And precisely freedom of religion, including legal freedom for Muslims to convert away from Islam, remains extremely difficult for traditional Islamic theology to accept. That is why serious discussion is needed.

Brutal civil wars and the plight of many hundreds of thousands of refugees have made an important question into an urgent question. Are Islam and democracy reconcilable? I truly hope so, but it would be foolish to think our dreams will all be reality.

Thomas K. Johnson, Ph.D.

Introduction

Why are there so few true democracies in countries shaped by Islam? Do democracy and Islam represent irreconcilable polar opposites? Does Islam forbid the introduction of democratic systems? Is the tension between Islam and democracy permanent and unchangeable? Or can one find within Islamic theology and history identifiable points of departure which could support a comprehensive justification and endorsement of democracy?

This question is not only relevant for the region known as the Middle East, where the predominant lack of democratic structures – with the exception of Turkey – is striking: *"Of the 47 Islamic states (those with a majority Muslim population), more than 90% of them are not free; 77% have to be regarded as dictatorships."*[2] This assessment from a decade ago cannot to be significantly revised even after the so-called of the "Arabellion."[3] The question which must be answered is whether Islam is directly responsible for this absence of democracy. To keep perspective, one must not forget that the most populous country shaped by Islam, Indonesia, is a true democracy. This is also the case with the predominantly Muslim country of Lebanon. Is it thus the case that social and political developments have not allowed democracy to gain a strong foothold in Arab countries? Furthermore, what would have to change so that in the MENA region,[4] that is to say, the Middle East and Northern Africa, true democracies could develop?

However, the question of the compatibility of democracy and Islam is not only significant for the Middle East and Northern Africa. The question is also relevant for Europe, where Muslims have lived in democratic societies for more than 50 years. Many greatly treasure the freedoms and advantages in Europe, including democratic structures, and prefer living in Western societies rather than in their countries of origin or, more specifically, the countries of origin of their ancestors. Many have become citizens

---

[2] Wolfgang Merkel, "Religion, Fundamentalismus und Demokratie," in Wolfgang Schluchter (ed.), *Fundamentalismus, Terrorismus, Krieg* (Weilerswist: Velbrück, 2003), pp. 61-85, quoted in Manfred Brocker and Tine Stein, "Einleitung," in Tine Stein (ed.), *Christentum und Demokratie* (Darmstadt: WGB, 2006), pp. 7-13, here p. 8.

[3] Compare, for instance, the survey "Democracy Index 2011. Democracy under Stress. A Report from the Economist Intelligence Unit." http://www.sida.se/Global/About%20Sida/Så%20arbetar%20vi/EIU_Democracy_Index_Dec2011.pdf (accessed December 18, 2012) and: *Freedom in the World 2012: The Arab Uprisings and their Global Repercussions.* http://www.freedomhouse.org/sites/default/files/FIW%202012%20Booklet_0.pdf (accessed December 18, 2012).

[4] MENA: Middle East and North Africa.

of European states. A number of their opinion leaders and theologians, however, have emphatically warned the Muslim minority in Europe against too high a degree of integration and participation in democratic processes. They call upon the Muslim minority to separate themselves and refuse to make Europe their ultimate home. In particular, the Salafists have stood out in the headlines with their strident rejection of democracy and Western society. Are Salafists able to invoke Islam for their judgment of democracy? What do the Koran, tradition, and Islamic theology have to say about the topic of democracy and legitimate rule?

Others who speak for the Muslim community, in contrast, affirm democracy as a principle which is authentically Islamic. Then, however, they only accept selected aspects of democracy into Islam while rejecting others, such as the freedom for Muslims to choose to convert away from Islam or the publication of cartoons of Mohammed. In the process, they co-opt democracy and reinterpret it until it fits into their predetermined interpretive framework. In a certain sense, they Islamize the Western understanding of democracy and modify it within the framework of their own concepts. They reject every aspect of democracy which, in their view, is not warranted by Islam. For them, democracy may only be what is useful to them (e.g., the freedom to propagate Islam), not, however, what contradicts a legal understanding shaped by Sharia law or Islamic law (such as Western freedom of the press, which includes the publication of caricatures of Mohammed). This reinterpreted concept of democracy is, at best, a mere fragment of true democracy.

Other Muslim intellectuals, theologians, and authors have drafted various models for unifying Islam with human rights, including real freedom and equality, as well as substantiating democracy on the basis of Islam. Upon which basis do they construct their arguments? Are their proposals signposts for the future? What is their meaning for established Islamic theology? And what are the preconditions which have to be established in order to help democracy be accepted and implemented in societies characterized by Islam?

I. Essential characteristics of a real democracy

The term "democracy," comprised of the word for "people" (Greek: demos) and for "rule" (Greek: kratos), stems from ancient Greece and stood for rule which directly went forth from the people and was exercised by the people. The high point of democracy, as it developed there, has primarily been set at the beginning of the fifth century B.C.[5] In the broadest sense, the term "democracy" designates a government put into a position of power according to the will of the majority of the people via free elections. It receives its legitimacy from the conscious expression of the people's will. In a democracy, the people comprise the actual responsible body for the authority of the state, and they charge their elected representatives with the formulation of a constitution and the configuration of a political system.

Democracies are characterized by a separation of powers into an executive branch (sometimes called "the government"), a legislative branch (a congress or parliament), and a judicial branch (which is independent from the other branches of government). Democracies act within the framework of a constitution which governs the actions of the state and respect the basic rights of the citizens as well as the rights of identified groups (especially religious communities). Among these rights are, above all, the rights of freedom of opinion, both politically and personally, freedom of the press, freedom of religion, and the freedom to organize. Democracies protect the right of minority political parties to exist and maneuver, as well as the possibility to freely voice their opinions and to peacefully change the balance of power.

What is expected of a democracy is that it embodies the rule of law, with the certainty that legal rights will be protected, in such a manner that representatives of the state are legally accountable for their actions. Furthermore, it is expected that these representatives adhere to prevailing law. In particular, true democracies grant their citizens the opportunity to peacefully dissolve government by a majority decision and to replace it with another via just, free, general, and secret elections.

---

[5] See Thomas Meyer, *Was ist Demokratie? Eine diskursive Einführung* (Wiesbaden: VS Verlag, 2009), p. 16.

Although there are diverging democratic theories within political science, there is a broad consensus that one of the most important preconditions for democracy is the equality and freedom of all the citizens: The fundamental equality of all people means, consequently, that all people are to be treated equally before the law. It also means that the same measure of rights and freedoms will be granted to them within the constitutional state. Citizens' freedom encompasses their freedom of self-determination, the freedom to form their own personal, political, and religious opinions, and the freedom to act out of their opinions in their participation in the political process. At the same time, it is also a freedom and, more specifically, a right to be protected from arbitrary state action and the violation of their rights. With that said, fundamental democratic rights are implemented, which according to content, are closely linked with the principles of freedom and equality. For the most part, these are set down in a constitution and are legally enforceable. Among the inalienable fundamental rights in Germany, for instance, are the protection of human dignity, the right to free development of one's personality, the right to physical integrity, the right to equal treatment for men and women, the freedom of belief, and the freedom of opinion, as well as the right to freely choose one's profession.

A. Do democracies have Christian roots?

A democracy is not a religiously legitimated form of rule or form of state. As a result, it cannot be deemed to be "Christian" *per se*. However, according to the opinion of many, it does possess a collection of characteristics which could be designated as the implementation of a number of foundational Christian principles, even if not all democracies – and this applies above all to Indonesia and Turkey – are culturally shaped by Christianity: *"Today, of a total of 88 free democracies, 79 of them, thus 90%, are majority Christian. Next to this there is one Jewish democracy and seven democracies which have Far Eastern religions representing the majority, whereby in Mauritius and in South Korea Christians make up a second large segment of the population."*[6] And yet the following applies: *"Christianity fits with democracy like a hand fits in a glove."*[7] This is because "liberal democracy," according to the notion of leading

---

[6]   Thomas Schirrmacher, "Demokratie und christliche Ethik," in *Aus Politik und Zeitgeschichte* 14/2009. http://www.bpb.de/apuz/32086/demokratie-und-christliche-ethik?p=all (December 18, 2012).

[7]   William J. Hoye, *Demokratie und Christentum: Die christliche Verantwortung für demokratische Prinzipien* (Münster: Aschendorff, 1999), p. 366.

representatives of Evangelical and Catholic churches, *"corresponds in a special way to the Christian view of humankind."*[8] This is the case even if Christians, as the same statement emphasizes, cannot *"expect the comprehensive realization of what is good or, as it were, the establishment of a perfect world free from problems"* from any form of government, or in other words, from *"any human action."*[9]

It is a basic Christian assumption that people are fallible and that power, therefore, can lead to the abuse of power. The attempt to limit the power of those who rule within democracy comes through the opportunity to vote all democratically elected representatives out of power. It is also expressed in the form of oversight bodies (such as parliaments). The principle of the general and equal right to vote, which allots to every citizen the same number of votes and the same weight to his or her voice, can be viewed as the political application of biblical thinking on the equality of all people before God. The similar principle, that the individual person is free before God in his decisions, and is therefore bound primarily to his own conscience and not to the consciences of other people, requires free and secret elections to prevent manipulation of the individual's voting decision. Therefore, there are prohibitions on one individual voting representatively for another and on deliberating with others in the voting booth.

A number of authors additionally mention the desacralizing of worldly rule, meaning a turning away from the notion that a quasi-divine and uncontested authority is manifested in worldly power. This is only possible if the human fallibility of the ruler is also truly recognized. According to this notion, there are no infallible and unquestionable god-kings who are not to be scrutinized. Rather, they are stewards in high places who may find themselves in need of correction. This corresponds with the biblical insight into the susceptibility of all people to temptations, as well as with the prohibition against placing people in the position of God. In particular, the idea of an emperor as god in Roman times is a cautionary example regarding the dangers for society when unlimited power is placed in the hands of a ruler who exercises authority similar to that of a god and is revered as a god. It is precisely against the emperor god-kings of the Romans to which Jesus directs his demand to separate worldly and religious spheres, to give

---

[8]   *Demokratie braucht Tugenden*. Gemeinsames Wort des Rates der Evangelischen Kirche in Deutschland und der Deutschen Bischofskonferenz zur Zukunft unseres demokratischen Gemeinwesens (Hannover/Bonn: Kirchenamt der EKD/Sekretariat der Deutschen Bischofskonferenz, 2006), p. 12.

[9]   Ibid., p. 14.

to God and to the emperor separately what properly belongs to each (Matthew 22:21).

The idea that the ruler finds himself in principle on the same plane as that of those who are ruled, such that he is not *per se* above the plane of the ruled, can definitely be viewed as the political implementation of the Christian view of humanity, in which every individual has the same inalienable image of God awarded to him or her. The accountability of those in power, in the sense responsibility to the community, could be understood as an application of the biblical principle according to which everyone, irrespective of the person, has to give an account of his stewardship before God and humankind (Luke 12:20).[10] The logical consequence of the image of God in humanity, of humanity's dignity and freedom, is humankind's freedom of conscience and freedom of religion. The inalienable dignity of humanity, which springs from humanity's *imago Dei* as a creation, protects individuals from coming under the complete grasp of others, thus protecting them *"from the state, society, the people, the consensus"*[11] and, with that said, protecting them from comprehensive monopolization and capture under totalitarian demands of thought and action without alternative courses of action.

B.   Would democracy be better served with a "Christian state?"

In Germany, the state as an institution is to adhere to neutrality in religious questions, even if the history and culture of Germany have been shaped by Christianity. Though a number of Christians seem to desire a "Christian state" which would represent and embody the Christian faith, it should be noted that such a state would then probably almost automatically see itself as a representative of the interests of one or both major churches (Catholic and Protestant) and offer them exclusive privileges. This would bring about disadvantages for other Christian denominations (such as Coptic or Greek Orthodox). Even if the state were to make itself the representative of all Christian denominations, there would be the remaining problem of demarcation: Who would define the boundary cases

---

[10]   Hans Maier defends the notion that the establishment of democratic constitutional states would not have been possible without Christianity. Hans Maier, *Demokratischer Verfassungsstaat ohne Christentum – Was wäre anders?* (St. Augustin/Berlin: Konrad-Adenauer-Stiftung, 2006).

[11]   As formulated by William J. Hoye, *Demokratie und Christentum. Die christliche Verantwortung für demokratische Prinzipien* (Münster: Aschendorff, 1999), p. 35.

as "Christian" or "non-Christian," to decide which group is a special type of Christian and which is a different religion? If this happened, the state would become a theological authority regarding the contents of the Christian faith. This has never been successful in the past.

For that reason, the state should preserve what could be called *"respectful non-identification"*[12] by acknowledging the right of all religious communities to development and expression, to a public presence, and to peaceful solicitation for new members.[13] Moreover, the state can enter into contractual relationships with religious communities which are set up for permanence and with representation as statutory bodies under public law (in German, Körperschaften des öffentlichen Rechts or KdöR), loyal to Germany's Foundational Law (constitution) whereby both sides profit. Partisanship on the part of the state for a certain religious community would suspend or severely limit the religious freedom and legal equality of non-Christian religious communities. Such action would not only be irreconcilable with the law; it would also be politically impossible in our country in which one-third of the population does not belong to either of the two major national churches (*Volkskirchen*) and where only a part of the remaining two-thirds of the citizens who are still official church members see themselves as convinced Christians. [Ed: The German word *Volkskirche* refers to the Protestant Church of Germany (EKD) and the Catholic Church of Germany; both have extensive cooperative agreements with the German government, partly resulting from their history, which are designed to serve selected public purposes within Germany today; neither is truly a "state church" in the sense of being state run or state endorsed.) Additionally, a question which remains open is how a Christian state would judge atheists, especially which privileges it would possibly withdraw from them on the basis of their lack of a faith confession; this would indicate an abrupt end to religious freedom.

A religiously neutral, democratic state does not face religious communities indifferently. Rather, in a multifaceted manner, such a state is dependent upon cooperation with religious communities. The state theorist and expert in constitutional law, Ernst-Wolfgang Böckenförde, in his famous "Böckenförde Dictum," formulated it as follows: *"The liberal, secular*

---

[12] According to Heiner Bielefeldt, *Muslime im säkularen Rechtsstaat: Integrationschancen durch Religionsfreiheit* (Bielefeld: Transcript, 2003), p. 23.

[13] See the comprehensive explanation on the relationship between the religiously neutral state and churches in Maria Pottmeyer, *Religiöse Kleidung in der öffentlichen Schule in Deutschland und England: Staatliche Neutralität und individuelle Rechte im Rechtsvergleich* (Tübingen: 2011), especially pp. 34ff; 148ff; 164ff; 178ff.

state lives on preconditions which it cannot itself guarantee."[14] This means that the state can pass laws imposing sanctions against murder and theft, but the state cannot ensure that the majority of the citizens will continue to judge murder and theft to be wrong. That is to say, the state cannot ensure that people will agree with a canon of values upon which state legislation is based. If a large portion of the population no longer agrees with this canon or platform of values and the legislation deriving from it, the democratic state can no longer enforce compliance with these laws. Therefore, the state encourages religious communities, to which it grants statutory corporate rights under certain preconditions, and with which it cooperates. For their part, religious communities support the state in the sense of developing and maintaining a canon of values in which they promote peace, law, and moral values, while acknowledging the state's monopoly on force and punishment. This cooperation between the state and religious communities is expressed in the tax exemption of donations, the giving of religious instruction (allowed in German public schools), or special regulations in labor law and social law.

The mutual relinquishment of power by the church and by the state within German culture was achieved through a tenacious struggle. On the one hand, state goodwill toward religious communities and state neutrality with respect to the content-based assessment of religious beliefs, on the other hand the foundational acknowledgment of the state monopoly on force and the state realm of control where the commandments of the church do not apply, have had far-reaching ramifications: the separation of powers and the allocation of separate spheres for religion and the state have led to the development of religious freedom, universal human rights, a type of secularism that is not necessarily anti-religious, the freedom to conduct research, and religious pluralism. This is the case even if, for a long time, there was suspicion on the part of churches in regard to democracy with civil rights and liberties. Both mainline churches (Protestant and Catholic) did not finally affirm democracy with full civil rights and liberties until the twentieth century, when they published position papers accepting democracy and religious diversity.

While the church only retains the position of a moral authority in a constitutional state, so that the church is no longer a lawmaking and political authority, the state, on the other hand, preserves neutrality and distance toward religions, so that no citizen of the state is forced to practice a religion or consider a religion to be true. The state, which no longer poses

---

[14]   Ernst-Wolfgang Böckenförde, *Staat, Gesellschaft, Freiheit* (Frankfurt: Suhrkamp, 1976), p. 60.

as a judge over religious content, does not force the representatives of religion to abandon their truth claims and take up the position of state neutrality. Reciprocally, representatives of religions can be expected to accept people as citizens of the state even if they think or believe differently and to accept legislation with a secular orientation. In this manner, the self-limitation of the state to the non-religious sphere makes reconciliation between churches and a secular state possible.

II. Democracy and Islam: irreconcilable?

As to the question of how capable countries shaped by Islam are of having democracy, it is not only a matter of the political circumstances in such states. It also has to do with which worldview foundations can be enlisted to justify democracy and civil rights and liberties: Which form of rule is allowed in Islam? Which form of government is considered by it to be ideal?

As is the case with many other questions, the text of the Koran gives very little in the way of concrete information as to how the political system was ordered at the time of Mohammed. The result is that one is hardly able to draw any precise directions for a form of rule which could be considered an ideal. Indeed, it could be concluded from Mohammed's role as a military leader, lawgiver, and prophet that the ideal Islamic form of rule should be one which is simultaneously spiritual and worldly. Above all, leaders from the Islamist spectrum, for instance, arguably the most influential Pakistani theologian, author, and politician Abu l-A'la Maududi (1903-1979), have propagated this form of rule as the sole legitimate form and have worked toward the implementation of this ideal with all their might.

However, with this thought it is primarily a matter of the unification of the state and religion in an ideal projected back onto Islamic history. In reality, throughout its entire history, beginning, at the latest, from the time after the rule of the four caliphs (632-661 A.D.) succeeding Mohammed, the Islamic community has had to grapple with the fact that it has never again had a single ruler over the entire population of Muslims wherein there has been a unification of worldly and spiritual power. Instead, the reality has been a number of rival families, dynasties, and theological groups. They have struggled and fiercely fought and bitterly wrestled for the claim to rule and, respectively, exercise interpretive sovereignty with respect to Islam. In the process, struggles within the Islamic community have not only shaped power politics but also theology.

As soon as the time immediately following Mohammed's death in 632 A.D., a foundational theological (and power politics-related) dispute broke out among Mohammed's adherents and intensified progressively over the course of centuries: At the latest, since 860 A.D. - the time of the momentously decisive battle of Karbala in present-day Iraq - the group known as Shiites has been seen as firmly established and the community of Muslims as essentially split. Over the centuries, Sunnis as well as Shiites have further split into numerous groupings and sub-groupings. While the caliphate had represented a certain unity of worldly and spiritual power under Mohammed's first four successors, in later centuries the increasingly strong denominational and power political split became a reality. There were caliphs and opposing caliphs, regional dynasties and special political groups who were intermittently successful (such as the Ishmaelite Fatimids) until the dramatic downfall of the Abbasid Caliphate at the time of the Mongolian invasion of Baghdad in 1258. After that, parts of the Middle East, the Balkans, and the Arabian Peninsula were ruled by the Ottoman Sultans from the thirteenth century until the founding of the Turkish Republic in 1923-1924. The Ottomans were of Turkic origin and had immigrated into present-day Turkey. Furthermore, they first converted to Islam in the course of this process. They were never accepted by many Arab scholars as legitimate Islamic rulers. From the first Islamic century onward, one can no longer speak about a unity between worldly and religious rule, about a uniform answer to the question of who is justified to rule the entire community of Muslims or even who is the proper official representative of all Muslims.

On the topic of the "recovery" of democracy in Islam, Muslim spokespeople have repeatedly pointed out that the Koran advocates advice for a ruler. Thus, there was the idea of the inclusion of a number of voices in the political decision-making process from the time of Mohammed onward. Suras 3:159 and 42:38 are cited most often in support of this point of view. They recommend that believing Muslims should mutually "consult" with each other. The term "to consult," which is used in the Koran in both verses, has the same root as the often-used term "shura" (consultation) in the Islamic political sphere. From the viewpoint of Islamic apologists, shura is a type of "Islamic democracy," which is said to have been established in the course of Islamic history.

It is indeed correct that throughout the history of Islam, the first four caliphs after Mohammed were the result of an election. However, beginning in 661 A.D., the Umayyad Dynasty made the caliphate hereditary. As Islamic historiography explains it, Mohammed most probably consulted with his confidants regarding military expeditions and peace agreements. Viewed realistically, neither in Islamic history nor in the present are there – at least in Arabic countries – elements of true democracy which are demonstrable according to the definition offered above. Today there are not even committees which effectively exercise control over the executive branch of government and would be even roughly comparable with a Western democratic parliament. Indeed, there are advisory committees in a number of countries, particularly in the Gulf States, which carry the title "majlis ash-shura" (consultative council or advising committee); nevertheless, the Gulf monarchies are absolute monarchs, and only influential families within the respective countries send representatives to their advisory committees. And these committees do not place limitations or control on the absolute power of the ruling families, make rulers accountable for violations of the law, or remove the rulers from power. The form of rule in the early days of Islam was the caliphate, and later it was autocracy, absolute monarchy, or an autocratic presidential system (a *de facto* omnipotent president with a rubber-stamp parliament), as well as a theocracy in a small number of cases. True democracies have not arisen in the Arabic realm up until now.

A.   The Arab Revolution: a pathway to democracy?

On December 17, 2010, in protest against harassment by the local police, the Tunisian greengrocer Mohamed Bouazizi doused himself with gasoline and set himself on fire in the market square of Sidi Bouzid. A few weeks later he succumbed to his injuries and died in the hospital. This desperate protest by an impoverished street vendor against the arbitrary treatment and continuous humiliation demonstrated by omnipotent authorities was the start of a wildfire of protests against the autocratic governments throughout the region. These events seized the large part of Northern Africa and the Middle East. Protests, rioting, strikes, demonstrations, and numerous acts of violence followed. Hundreds of thousands of people went out on the streets and into public places. Police and military forces loyal to the government were deployed and abused the demonstrators with water cannons in various locations; they threatened, bludgeoned, arrested, and injured the demonstrators, hitting some with gunfire, leading to the deaths of many. None of these actions was able to silence the protests or to permanently intimidate the protesters and keep them from further demonstrations. There were also many women who participated courageously in the protest movements, although government forces also moved against them, and many of them were publicly humiliated, arrested, and beaten.

The most important concern people had during the "Arabellion" was the desire for freedom from the ubiquitous oppression of corrupt regimes within Arab countries. Until then, the regimes had variously been characterized by secularism (e.g., in Tunisia), dominated by the military (e.g., in Egypt), dominated by a single ruling dynasty (e.g., in Syria), or paraded themselves primarily as alleged religious rule (e.g., in Saudi Arabia). In a number of countries, people were largely looking for reforms. For instance, King Mohammed VI of Morocco is an extremely popular monarch who even invokes Mohammed, the founder of Islam, in his lineage as part of his legitimacy; in recent years he has implemented a number of reforms in Morocco. These reforms have brought a breath of freedom into the country. In other countries, for instance in Tunisia or Egypt, protesters called for the immediate relinquishment of power by the tyrants and for the overthrow of the regime.

Causes of the revolution: a lack of civil liberties and a lack of future prospects

An extremely important factor for understanding the Arab Spring has to do with demographic developments in the region: The percentage of the population under the age of 25 is near to 50% in many countries. In Yemen, this percentage is approximately 65%.

These youth have, for the most part, lived in societies which have offered them few if any prospects for the future because of numerous prohibitions and restrictions. The unemployment rate is immense everywhere; among youth it is frequently at levels of 30-40%, and in certain locations it can be as high as 70%. However, attractive jobs and affordable housing – the preconditions for starting a family – as well as public space for helping shape and participate in society, including personal freedoms in art, culture, religious affiliation, and political forums, are all scarcely present.

These young people have grown up under repressive regimes and possess few civil rights and liberties. They view themselves as observers or even losers in the twenty-first century's globalization and affluence, who in spite of natural resources, such as natural gas and oil, have seen these developments pass them by. In a number of regions, the population is growing so quickly that it swallows up any economic growth, and neither schools nor the building of new residential structures, neither the labor market nor the universities, have been able to keep up. The result is that in many Islamic societies there are armies of academics who are unemployed and have no prospects. In other countries there are countless unqualified people who are unemployed and for whom there are few possibilities for feeding their family other than being active in the meager agricultural sector.

Adverse economic developments

Over the past 20 years, hundreds of thousands of impoverished agricultural laborers everywhere in this region have migrated to the large cities. There they live in the fast-growing poor and slum districts without hope of education for their children and advancement of their social status. Thus, they build an army of discontents who desire to see fast change. At the same time, the issue of ensuring that the population has basic foods from national production has been aggravated, given the extent of migration from the country to the city. With a rapidly growing population, the state has been forced to continue purchasing wheat on the world market and subsidizing basic foodstuffs.

Until now the Arab countries have comprised a region with dramatic economic weakness and comparatively low productivity. This is the case in spite of what is in many places the presence of valuable natural resources. Thus, the economies of Asia have been growing at an average of some 5% per year, while the Arab states have been experiencing growth of only 0.2%. This means that economic growth is less than population growth. The result is the use of state resources for subsidies and a lower standard of living for the majority of the population. Arab states primarily finance their existence with state benefits – for example, in Egypt through income from the Suez Canal – through tourism, through oil production, as well as through financial transfers from Egyptian citizens working in the Emirates or living in Saudi Arabia. Even the abundantly available natural resources such as petroleum and natural gas have hardly contributed to the economic development of the region, for the earnings from these resources have, up to now, in large part not been employed for the development of the infrastructure and have thus not reached the population. Frequently, revenues from natural resources are distributed by potentates to members of a small elite and their protégés, such as high-ranking military or tribal leaders, who receive privileges and benefits in return for supporting the ruler. For that reason, relatively few jobs have come from petroleum and natural gas exploration, and efficient local processing of natural resources is a frequent problem: Thus, oil-rich Iran has had to import gasoline to the present day because there are not enough oil refineries in Iran to process the available petroleum.

Corruption and oppression

Additionally, rampant corruption and patronage systems prevent any sort of development. On the whole, as participants in the revolutions depicted the situation, young workers do not advance through their own work and achievement in these societies. Instead, it is through being in the right family and through relationships, or because of power structures, as well as tribal and patron-client relationships. These factors stifle all creativity and all independent entrepreneurial action and produce social inequality and injustice.

Additionally, there are the extremely inefficient state institutions, authoritarianism, tyranny, legal insecurity, and an excessive bureaucracy. Restrictive minority and women's rights are also well-known problems in Arab societies. This lack of rights has an effect on social development. Given the authoritarianism, the strong influence exerted by conservative theologians all the way into the heart of society (particularly in Iran and Saudi Arabia), as well as the cultural and religiously justified limitation on women's rights, improvement for women in legal regulations has only been gradual in individual countries. Among these improvements is the increase in the marriageable age or in making divorce easier. However, success in achieving legal equality for women up to now has not been resounding. In Arab societies, only a relatively few women in the privileged upper class have good opportunities for professional fulfillment. The majority of women have to get along with only slight opportunities for personal and professional development and have to accept social and legal disadvantages. The same applies for minorities: They are not completely without rights, but socially they are discriminated against everywhere and are excluded from participating in public offices and from achieving higher positions in many places. However, when women and minorities have their rights curtailed, are discriminated against, and are bullied, while those who can work find too little employment, the region cannot develop, especially if the population is growing rapidly at the same time.

The dreadful state of education is an additional factor which inhibits the development of Arab societies and leads to poverty and dissatisfaction, with a resulting perceived lack of prospects. In a number of states, such as Egypt and Algeria, 30% of the population cannot read or write. In Mauritania, Morocco, and Yemen, the number approaches 50%. Among women the rate lies significantly higher. Across the country of Yemen on the whole, the average is surely 70-75%. Immense population growth amplifies the education problem. In turn, a lack of education inhibits economic development, entrepreneurship, and the ability to take individual responsibility. Such illiteracy increases dependency on government services. This educational poverty produces further gateways for religious radicalism. Beyond that, there is a type of correlation between the lack of education and the omnipotent secret intelligent apparatuses and tyrannical legal systems which are widely to be found; in many places police and other security forces use systematic torture, joined with corruption and nepotism, which would be more difficult to impose if the populace were well educated. After the people had freed themselves from their colonial lords in the twentieth century, it seems that their descendants lost their dignity to the new rulers in Arab countries, so that the people now face oppression, tyranny, and a lack of opportunities for codetermination and political freedom of expression. The people tried to regain this dignity through the Arabellion.

B.   Why were Islamists voted into office?

"Islam can also do democracy!" This was the way the press enthusiastically titled the beginning of the Arabellion. In part, the Western media concluded all too soon that Arab countries were on the verge of an imminent change to a comprehensive introduction of democracy with civil rights and liberties – possibly even a liberal society. At the latest, it became clear after the parliamentary elections in Egypt in 2012 that this was a misperception by the media: at least in Egypt, the call for freedom and the end of tyranny were not synonymous with the wish for the introduction of a secular legal and governmental system and a separation of religion and the state according to the Western model. On the contrary: more than 70% of the votes in Egypt were for Islamist parties such as the Freedom and Justice Party of the politico-religious movement called the Muslim Brotherhood, and for the extreme Islamist party Light of the Salafists – even if one can not conclude that these 70% voters were Islamists; many were just opting for an alternative to the authoritarian regimes of the past. But the introduction of a legal system and government which could even remotely be designated as secular lies in the far distance. The development in Tunisia is not as dramatic, but the 2011 election of the Islamic Ennahda party under the leadership of Rashid al-Ghannouchi to lead a coalition government in the first place had raised concerns that Tunisia's orientation might differ only slightly from that of Egypt. But the question remains: Why did the Egyptian and Tunisian populations not initially see themselves as best served by more secularly oriented politicians?

In order to explain this, one must first be reminded that the western assessment of the circumstances will vary greatly from those in the Middle East. As a general rule, we Europeans view Egypt as an "Islamic" country, which has long been influenced by the commands of Islam and Sharia law in its legislation. With that said, from our point of view, the "Islam" factor cannot be effectively separated from the oppression of people in recent decades. On the other hand, many people in the Middle East would point out, conversely, that the earlier Egyptian regime under President Husni Mubarak dates back to the Cold War and was in no sense an Islamic regime. They would emphasize that Islamist groups were at best tolerated in recent decades, and many were severely oppressed. Moreover, Egypt's legislation was only oriented toward Sharia law in a few areas, even if the constitution of Egypt alluded to Sharia law as an overarching principle. Many people in Egypt would, for that reason, tend to deny that they lived in an "Islamic state" prior to the revolution. However, they lived in a state which deprived them of their fundamental civil rights and liberties, challenged human and women's rights, and allowed many citizens to arbitrarily become the victims of violence, humiliation, and the deprivation of liberty. Since, as a rule, the Islam of believing Muslims has counted as a synonym for justice and a satisfactory measure of civil rights and liberties, which is frequently viewed as superior to Western notions of human rights, many people attributed the defects in Egypt to "too little" Islam and not to "too much." Something also to be taken into consideration is the general trend of increasing Islamization of Islamic societies from northern Africa to Asia over the past 30 years. Thus, rulers such as Husni Mubarak in Egypt or Ben Ali in Tunisia, whose accession to power occurred at the time of the East-West conflict, were not perceived in terms of being "Islamic" in the sense of being just and legitimate. Rather, they were judged by many of their citizens to be secular. Indeed, they were even decried by some as godless.

One must also keep in view that Western societies and their civil rights and liberties are by no means considered exemplary and desirable by a majority. Many in the Middle East see the West as having an inimical attitude toward Islam and as being morally adrift. The recently fought wars in Iraq and Afghanistan have demonstrated to them that the West measures its politics and human rights questions by a double standard and is only interested in its own economic interests. For that reason, it is not surprising that a majority of the population decided at the ballot box for a more strongly Islamist-oriented government. Additionally, Islamic and Islamist movements, the Egyptian Muslim Brotherhood being an example of the latter, have in particular provided the poor with social support throughout the decades. In a country in which public assistance, healthcare, and educational programs are often not sufficiently available, aid programs have enormous reverberation.

C. Are democracies emerging in the Middle East?

Free elections were held in Egypt and Tunisia after the revolution. Can one conclude from this that democracy has already arrived on the scene in the Middle East? Hardly. And yet it seems natural to many people in the Middle East that their Islamic faith does not stand in the way of their desire for increased civil rights and liberties. According to the notion many people have in the Middle East, Islam and democracy can surely be unified, for a government and legal system characterized by secularism is, from their point of view, neither a guarantee nor a condition of democracy. Their experiences with governments characterized by secularism in the last decades have confirmed them in this point of view. And if it is determined by them that the Koran and the Islamic tradition (the reports regarding the acts and sayings of Mohammed as well as of his immediate successors) contain no detailed directions for a system of government, such that the sources of Islam provide neither a foundation for a constitution nor a system of laws, then that is absolutely appropriate. Why should Islam and democracy not be able to work together?

Even if some elected Islamist rulers, such as the Muslim Brotherhood in Egypt, have never deviated from their manifesto and basic program over the entire 85 years of their existence, which is to bring about the complete application of Sharia law (including the drastic corporal punishments), the question has to be asked whether they now want to moderate this claim and if they still wish to apply Sharia law fully. The majority of the people were surely hoping for a tempered Islamic government which would give them more justice, human dignity, and freedom for self-development. Most Egyptians do not want to live in a Sharia state. They desire to see neither the introduction of a religious police force nor the punishment of having one's hand cut off for committing a theft. However, how will the political structure look instead of that? Will the present limitations on polygamy remain in place, and will women be able to defend the rights they have had up to now? For example, will women be able to defend their right to initiate a divorce? The rights women have had up to now are viewed as un-Islamic in the eyes of many Islamists. Which rights do minorities receive in a state ruled by Islamists? Where do personal civil rights and liberties end? How does the future of religious freedom look?

A particular set of problematic issues with respect to Islam consists in the fact that from the outset, law is so very closely associated with theology. A form of law particularly characterized by secularism is interpreted by many Islamists, both within the government as well as outside the gov-

ernment, as a betrayal of Islam. Other Egyptians, who fear that their freedoms could be lost under an Islamist government, have called for a secular
form of government and a civil society constitution. But even among them,
there has not necessarily been the thought of a liberal order with comprehensive religious freedom and an absence of state coercion. At the present,
there are not even majorities favoring a secular form of state, and the opposition is fragmented. Furthermore, after suddenly achieving freedoms,
such citizens were not able to organize themselves sufficiently in the short
time up to the elections, while the Muslim Brotherhood had a network for
85 years and was known to the majority of the population as a friend in
times of need.

Could Sharia law be kept under a present Islamist government but
moderately interpreted? Could it be the foundation for faith and life for
people and a standard for socio-political order without forming a Sharia
state such as in Saudi Arabia or Iran? In order for this to be the case, a
historic examination of Sharia law is necessary, which, for instance, would
divide its contents into eternally valid elements (e.g., commands relating
to fasting or prayer, which are also components of the legal framework of
Sharia law) and components which are historically limited in their validity
(e.g., the penal code). Individual Muslim scholars, such as Abdullahi an-
Na'im (b. 1946), who teaches in the US and comes from Sudan, have indeed
suggested a present-day demarcation regarding the validity of the Islamic
penal code as a way to an Islam which is humane and capable of living in
peace. However, up to now such scholars have not received a hearing from
the theological establishment, let alone are they finding groups of supporters. For a historicizing of the penal and socio-political components of
Sharia law, new patterns of interpretation have to be worked out, with the
help of which Sharia law could be reconciled with civil liberties and human
rights. Indeed, Sharia law is in principle flexible and interpretable, but its
basic interpretation is largely set down because up to today, what is viewed
as binding is the interpretive framework of legal scholars up to the tenth
century. According to this, it would, for example, not be possible to justify
the abolishment of polygamy, the legal equality of men and women, or the
legal equality of Muslims and non-Muslims.

D. Points of conflict between Islamic legal systems and democracy

Can societies shaped by Islam be democratic? In practice, this has hardly
been the case. But does the reason lie in the "Islam factor," or are the

causes primarily of a political and a social nature? It is well known that, as far as human rights and civil liberties are concerned, in societies characterized by Islam in the Middle East, things are in poor shape. Is the reason "too little" Islam, and are the circumstances traceable back to the misuse of power and mechanisms of oppression? Or is it rather that Islam is to be viewed as the cause of the serious human rights deficit?

In this context, it is essential to define what is to be understood by "Islam." For instance, is it the mere membership a majority of the population has in a religion, the traditional religiosity of most people, the social order characterized by Islam, the civil law as influenced by Sharia law, or is it the reference made in constitutions by most countries in the region to Sharia law as the source of all legislation?

Turkey represented a special case in the Middle East with its democratic orientation till things were changing. For that reason, many hopes for a democratically oriented Middle East were directed at Turkey. It served as a role model as one of the countries characterized by Islam with a moderate Islamic government. The economy was booming, and progress was being demonstrated in questions of human rights and religious freedom. Today, considerable changes related to human and freedom rights have become obvious.

A decisive difference between Turkey and the Arab countries consists in the attitude taken toward Sharia law. It was almost a century ago that Turkey disconnected itself from Sharia law as a legal system in the wake of the formation of the Turkish Republic in 1923-1924. It introduced a form of marital and family law which was completely characterized by secular notions following the model of Swiss civil law. It is for this reason that Turkey is the only country in the Middle East in which polygamy is forbidden by law. Only in similarly largely secularized Tunisia does one find that polygamy was also prohibited in the middle of the twentieth century. In penal law Sharia law has no meaning, and there are no legal sanctions against converting away from Islam. This is the case even if a person converting away from Islam must expect strong discrimination in the social realm. This development, which is specific to Turkey since the 1920s, appears to be hardly imaginable for Arabic countries at the present time: When President Recep Tayyip Erdoğan, upon the occasion of his visit to Egypt at the end of 2011, promoted a secular state with a separation between the state and religion, he encountered much criticism and rejection from the Egyptian side.[15]

---

[15]   See, for instance, the assessment of the Konrad-Adenauer-Stiftung, "Nur wenige Ägypter teilen Erdogans Haltung." (translation: "There are only a few Egyptians

Can "Islam," or more precisely stated, can a legal system shaped by religion, which is oriented toward religious norms for the authority of its civil law, guarantee equal civil rights and liberties to all people or even enable a peaceful change of power after a majority vote? "Islam" as something exercised privately or as an ethical structure of values will hardly be able to oppose democracy. There is no reason to assume that the exercise of Islam as a religion, e.g., through prayer and fasting, should stand in irreconcilable discord with democracy. However, this only applies with respect to Islam as a personal faith and not with respect to Islam as a legal system determining laws, values, and norms. Wherever Sharia law shapes law, the social order, and the dispensation of justice, there will be no comprehensive civil rights allowed in the sense of the 1948 UN Universal Declaration of Human Rights. The reason for this is that according to the traditional understanding, Sharia law cannot award equal rights to men and women, nor to Muslims and non-Muslims, nor to converts away from Islam and atheists. For that reason, with respect to an Islamic society where Sharia norms shape the legal system, there are sizeable difficulties along the path to democracy. This applies to the areas of marital and family law, in regard to comprehensive human rights, penal law, and especially the realms of freedom of thought, freedom of conscience, and freedom of religion.

Human rights and civil liberties

In order to prevent the emergence of a one-sided picture, it must be emphasized that there are already many organizations and individuals who are making efforts to improve the human rights situation in countries shaped by Islam. Frequently, they are making these efforts under very difficult conditions. Legal experts, intellectuals, writers, and journalists dedicatedly tout a principally new orientation in the human rights and democracy debate, while others advocate a practical way toward an improvement in the human rights situation. The latter do so by publicly – today particularly, via the internet – drawing attention to the abuse of power, tyranny, and concrete occurrences of injustice. Their work extends to support for those affected (victims of torture, the incarcerated, victims of arbitrary actions) as well as to raising public awareness. There are several hundred human rights organizations with various orientations, of various sizes, financial resources, and ways of operating, which frequently

---

who share Erdogan's stance.") http://www.kas.de/wf/de/33.29819/ (accessed December 18, 2012).

work through the respective governments and pursue diverse goals in the face of massive hindrances in the countries shaped by Islam. Large and well-known organizations are, for instance, the Arab Organization for Human Rights (AOHR), which was founded on December 1, 1983, in Limassol, Cyprus. This organization, which today has its head office in Cairo, serves as an umbrella organization for various regional human rights organizations. There are offshoots and partner organizations of the AOHR which have been started in Morocco, Algeria, Tunisia, Jordan, Bahrain, Kuwait, Lebanon and Yemen.[16] The goal of the AOHR is to advocate human rights for all the inhabitants of the Arab countries on the basis of the Universal Declaration of Human Rights. Particularly within the focus of this work are those who, according to UN stipulations, are unjustly imprisoned or are threatened with or affected by restrictions and forms of repression owing to their religion, gender, political convictions, race, skin color, or language. AOHR's work is concentrated on efforts to free political prisoners, to defend them, to support their family members, and where direct intervention is not possible, to observe and document human rights infringements through publications, conferences, and seminars.[17]

An additional large organization is the Egyptian Organization for Human Rights (EOHR), one of the oldest non-governmental organizations cooperating with the UN. The globally linked EOHR seizes upon the opportunity to exercise a watchdog function for the protection of human rights in Egypt and actively advocates the realization of expanded human rights.[18] However, it was not until after a tough battle that the EOHR received state recognition from the Egyptian Ministry of Social Affairs in 2003; it did not become a legally operating non-governmental organization (NGO) until 18 years after its founding. The EOHR is dedicated to documenting human rights violations in Egypt, independent of the identity of the victim or the culprit, and to lodging complaints, indeed even when the responsible party for the human rights violation is a representative of the state or in cases in which it involves private individuals. EOHR reports document cases of torture and abuse, and an additional focus of EOHR's activity is documenting discrimination against women and the support of refugees. Furthermore, through public relations work, the EOHR attempts to

---

[16] Carsten Jürgensen, "Die Menschenrechtsdebatte," in Sigrid Faath (ed.), *Politische und gesellschaftliche Debatten in Nordafrika, Nah- und Mittelost* (Hamburg: Deutsches Orient-Institut, 2004), pp. 295-318, here p. 296.

[17] See the self-portrayal: The Arab Organization for Human Rights: http://www.aohr.net/ (accessed November 5, 2012).

[18] See the self-portrayal: The Egyptian Organization for Human Rights: http://en.eohr.org/ (accessed December 18, 2012).

produce public awareness of the problem at hand, and by recruiting partners from among private institutions, it attempts to win supporters for its
cause. The EOHR mentions one of its goals to be "to reform the Egyptian
constitution and legislation" so that they are brought into accordance with
international human rights conventions and to press for an independent
judiciary, as well as the abolishment of discrimination on the basis of religious affiliation.[19] It is apparent from this that the EOHR has recognized
the actual problem in the religiously oriented legal system of Egypt, which
is rooted in Sharia law. If this value and norm-providing substructure is
not capped, or at least not pruned in its significance through historicizing
its application, it will only be with serious difficulty that human rights and
civil liberties achieve greater space in Egyptian society where these are not
provided for by Sharia law.

Islamic human rights declarations

There is another side running parallel to these human rights organizations: Islamic human rights organizations which really have more to do
with challenging rights than with guaranteeing them. Indeed, there is no
Islamic human rights declaration which has experienced universal recognition in countries shaped by Islam or which has been cast into concrete
legal texts and therefore has a binding effect according to international
law, such as is the case with the 1948 UN Universal Declaration of Human
Rights. A number of Islamic human rights declarations have achieved su-
pra-regional significance. Among them, there are two declarations which
are particularly prominent, the so-called Cairo Declaration on Human
Rights dating from 1990[20], as well as the Universal Islamic Declaration of
Human Rights issued in 1981.[21]

The Universal Islamic Declaration of Human Rights, dated September
19, 1981, comes from the pen of the Islamic Council of Europe, a non-governmental organization with its headquarters in London. The Islamic
Council of Europe, as a private institution, cannot claim any particular
type of following. The Declaration arose out of an initiative by the Saudi
royal house and was subject to the influential participation of scholars

---

[19]   http://en.eohr.org/about/ (accessed December 18, 2012).
[20]   See the text: http://www.dailytalk.ch/wp-content/uploads/Kairoer%20Erklae
       rung%20der%20OIC.pdf (accessed 18.12.2012).
[21]   See the text: http://www.way-to-allah.com/dokument/Internationale%20Men
       schenrechte-Deklaration%20im%20Islam.pdf (accessed December 18, 2012).

coming from Sudan, Pakistan, and Egypt.[22] Whoever studies the text of this document will be initially struck by the fact that this declaration was composed for Muslims (*"Therefore we, as Muslims, who believe ..."*). *One finds here that human rights are traceable back to Islam in a unilinear manner and are justified by Islam and laid claim to by Islam. As early as the preamble, one finds the following: "Islam gave to mankind an ideal code of human rights fourteen centuries ago. These rights aim at conferring honour and dignity on mankind and eliminating exploitation, oppression and injustice."*[23]

In the entire text, Islam is absolutely set forth as the "true religion," under which leadership alone it is possible for human reason to cope with this life. Furthermore, the preamble emphasizes the inviolability of Sharia law and the fact that Sharia law cannot be repealed, the duty of rulers to implement Sharia law, the necessity for a homogeneous society which will be achieved when everyone confesses religious devotion (to the Islamic religion), as well as the assurance of "security, dignity and liberty ... within the limits set by the Law" for every individual. This will be achieved through the complete implementation of Sharia law. The 23 Articles that follow are also a matter of explaining in more detail the form of life which is based solely upon Sharia law. The rights to life and freedom (Articles 1 and 2) and the equality of all people (Article 3) are important subjects. (In the German translation of the declaration, it was added to Article 3 that equality, however, is limited by pointing out that "devotion" – meaning affiliation with Islam – allows one individual to be given a priority over another. This means that there is a hierarchy within humanity according to religious confession.) Article 4 gives all individuals the right to be judged "in accordance with the Law" and to reject everything which opposes the law, which here means Sharia law. In Article 11 the issue is participation in public life, by which all Muslims are given the right to "assume public office ... subject to the Law." Conversely, one could conjecture that non-Muslims are either limited in their access to such offices or are refused the right to assume such offices. Article 12 guarantees the freedoms of belief, thought, and speech, which are likewise limited by the corresponding Sharia regulations. Thus, soliciting among Muslims for a faith other than Islam is forbidden. It condemns falling away from Islam and even prosecutes it. The same applies more generally to disloyal conduct toward the state, the

---

[22] According to Anne Duncker, *Menschenrechte im Islam: Eine Analyse islamischer Erklärungen über die Menschenrechte* (Berlin: Wissenschaftlicher Verlag, 2006), p. 27.

[23] *Allgemeine Erklärung der Menschenrechte im Islam* (*Universal Islamic Declaration of Human Rights*)   http://www1.umn.edu/humanrts/instree/islamic_declaration_HR.html (accessed 17.08.2015), p. 1.

authorities, and (the Islamic) religion: *"No one, however, is entitled to dissem-inate falsehood or to circulate reports which may outrage public decency, or to in-dulge in slander, innuendo or to cast defamatory aspersions on other persons."*

A more prominent declaration, the Cairo Declaration on Human Rights, was adopted on August 4, 1990, by 45 foreign ministers from a total of 57 member states of the Organization of Islamic Cooperation (OIC).[24] The OIC was founded on September 25, 1969, in Rabat. On the day following the adoption of the Declaration, August 5, 1990, it was handed over to the United Nations High Commissioner for Human Rights.[25] The Cairo Decla-ration on Human Rights declares Sharia law to be the sole foundation for granting human rights. Above and beyond that, the Cairo Declaration re-jects Western human rights declarations, such as the Universal Declara-tion of Human Rights of 1948, as a Judeo-Christian construct of secular and, for that reason, man-made laws. The Cairo Declaration on Human Rights does not deal with the tolerance and recognition of non-Muslims in any straightforward way. Rather, it is a call for Islamic dominance, which is justified by the revelation of Islam. This is made clear in the preamble, which emphasizes, in line with Sura 3.110, that *"the Islamic Ummah [the Mus-lim world community] which God made the best nation ... has given mankind a universal and well-balanced civilization."*[26] The preamble explains that the OIC would like to make its contribution so that people have a *"right to a dignified life in accordance with the Islamic Shari'ah"* – which immediately prompts the question of whether a life which is not in accordance with Sharia law can likewise be a *"dignified life."* In conclusion, the introduction underscores the divine, eternal character of Sharia law. Thus, it is warned that in Islam the rights and freedoms conferred may neither be rescinded nor infringed nor disregarded, for that is *"an abominable sin."*[27] In Articles 24 and 25 of the Cairo Declaration, the highest principle for interpreting human rights declarations is clarified: *"All the rights and freedoms stipulated in this Declara-tion are subject to the Islamic Shari'ah"* (Article 24), and in Article 25 it is stated more generally: *"The Islamic Shari'ah is the only source of reference for the explanation or clarification of any of the articles of this Declaration."*

This interpretive principle of the superordinate nature of Sharia law is clear in all the remaining 23 Articles of the Declaration. Thus, in Article 1 it is emphasized that all people are *"equal in terms of basic human dignity and*

---

[24] The OIC is closely linked to the Muslim World League in Mecca (http://www.mus limworldleague.org/mwlwbsite_eng/index.htm) (accessed December 18, 2012).

[25] According to Anne Duncker, *Menschenrechte im Islam*, p. 62.

[26] *Kairoer Erklärung der Menschenrechte* (*The Cairo Declaration on Human Rights in Islam*) http://www.oic-oci.org/english/article/human.htm (accessed 17.08.2015), p. 1.

[27] Ibid.

basic obligations and responsibilities." However, what remains striking is that there is no mention of the same rights as those mentioned in the 1948 Universal Declaration of Human Rights issued by the United Nations. Additionally, the Cairo Declaration supplements this with the statement that "*the true religion is the guarantee for enhancing such dignity.*" The urgent question that arises here is whether this dignity can only possibly be achieved if the "true religion" (of Islam) is accepted. This at least appears to be suggested in Article 1b, where one reads, "*... no one has superiority over another except on the basis of piety and good deeds.*" Piety and good deeds are named in the Koran at numerous points as a characteristic of true (Islamic) belief and the fulfillment of (Islamic) duties of faith (compare, for example, Sura 19:96). Likewise, the protection of and the integrity of human life are limited by Sharia law in Article 2a: "*It is prohibited to take away life except for a Shari'ah prescribed reason.*" According to Sharia law, for example, the taking of someone's life is provided for in cases of adultery and falling away from the faith of Islam (apostasy). In the Cairo Declaration Sharia law is raised above all worldly legislation and receives priority over it. With respect to women's equality, the Cairo Declaration notes that women should not be restrained from marriage on the basis of "*restrictions stemming from race, color, or nationality*" (Article 5). The free choice of a marriage partner independent of his or her religion is not mentioned. This reflects the provisions of Sharia law, namely, that according to the classical interpretation of Sharia law, a Muslim woman is not allowed to marry a non-Muslim man. Furthermore, it only says that women are "*equal to man in human dignity,*" – but apparently not when it comes to rights, which is not possible according to the stipulations of Sharia law. This is because of the idea that under Sharia law – at least when it comes to its traditional and completely overwhelming interpretation – there is no equality for women in terms of estate law, marital law, or divorce law.

What is problematic about these human rights declarations is the absolutizing of classical Sharia law and the elevation of Islam to the position of the sole true religion and way of life. The vague formulations which elucidate declarations of intent more than enforceable rights are also problematic. People receive rights only on the basis of their religious beliefs, full rights only as a Muslim, and more rights as a man than as a woman. A Muslim woman, in turn, has more rights than a non-Muslim man. However, when it comes to a Muslim man's freedom of expression and freedom of conscience, his rights are severely restricted according to Sharia law. When it comes to questions of conversion to another religion, an individual also loses rights confirmed by Sharia law if he damages society through his "disloyal" behavior. Likewise, human rights, as they are so defined, cannot be assigned to their full extent to atheists or those who think differently.

There are certainly significant human rights, such as the equality of all people and the legal equality of men and women, which are missing in both of these declarations. In like manner, a general and comprehensive acknowledgement of complete (including negative) freedom of religion and freedom of conscience, as well as the acknowledgement of the unhindered and public freedom to practice a religion or worldview, are totally missing. Furthermore, there is neither an acknowledgement of comprehensive civil rights, nor of rights to form a political will, nor of the equality of all people beyond the borders of the 'umma' (the community of all Muslims). Problematic issues concerning these declarations also relate to corporal punishment. Examples decreed in Sharia penal law are the amputation of the hand and foot in the case of theft or lashings and stoning, respectively, in the case of sexual offenses and adultery. One searches in vain for a condemnation of or distancing from these elements. Indeed, these forms of corporal punishment are currently applied in only a very few Islamic countries. However, their theoretical claim to validity is maintained by significant theologians at influential Islamic institutes of learning to this day. As a general rule, the claim to validity comes with the limitation that it may only be applied in a truly Islamic state. Owing to the necessity of a worldview justification for the granting of civil rights and liberties, the question arises as to how Islamist rulers in post-revolution Egypt (and other Middle East countries), who, according to their orientation to this time, should be labeled as advocates of Sharia law, want to concretely shape their human rights policy and gender policy regarding the status of women. A justification for equal rights and freedom rights will be difficult for them if they hold to a classical interpretation of Sharia law, but moving away from these norms in an official or public manner is also very difficult, since such a step may be perceived as apostasy.

Women's rights

Women's rights, as they are defined by Sharia law, present a problem as they relate to an international human rights perspective: they not only define the religious position of women before God; they also include a list of instructions relating to their social position, to estate law, and to marital law, which make equal legal status in society impossible. For that reason, the question to be asked as it relates to women's rights is whether Egypt, Tunisia, or other countries with Islamist-oriented governments, could decide for the implementation of equal rights (thus taking clear steps to do away with certain women's rights as defined by Sharia law) or whether a strict legislative orientation for family law which follows Sharia law will be pursued. Either decision could cause problems for those in power.

Sharia law relating to marital legal issues, as currently applied in the case of Egyptian civil law, codifies legal discrimination against women as an eternal, God-given order of things. Additionally, Sharia provisions for marriage and family are bound with local cultural norms and established traditions. They were already partly rooted in Arab tribal society and were integrated into the religion of Islam as it developed. Thus, a number of the generally acknowledged norms of behavior are a mixture of culture, religion, and tradition.

Marital law and family law, as these have been shaped by Sharia law, disadvantage women in a multiplicity of ways. One finds, for example, that it is the right of a man to punish his wife by neglecting her or chastising her in the case of her disobedience. This is anchored in Sura 4:34 and, according to the predominant opinion, affirmed by contemporary theologians and even largely accepted by society. In addition to a disadvantaged status in estate law and witness rights, a woman is also on worse footing than is a man when it comes to marital law, divorce law, and child custody. According to predominant opinion, the Koran allows a man to be married to up to four women and to have an unspecified number of concubines (Sura 4:3). Though traditional divorce proceedings allow the husband to divorce his wife by speaking a particular phrase of divorce ("I divorce you"), without requiring a justification or court proceedings, a number of Islamic countries which have made this process more difficult by prescribing a legal attempt at reconciliation. For her part, the wife, however, always requires court proceedings for divorce and can only receive a divorce if she is able to demonstrate serious misconduct on the part of her husband. Additionally, a divorce frequently leaves her without means, since her husband at most has to pay a few months of financial support. She is also often robbed of her children, who according to Sharia law, always belong to the family of the father after they have passed beyond the age of infancy.

Why has it been so difficult for women's rights, equal rights, and civil liberties to establish themselves in many countries shaped by Islam up to now? The women's movements in several Arab countries have fought courageously for progress and have made some achievements: raising the marriageable age, making it more difficult to divorce, and making it more difficult for a man to have multiple wives. At the same time, there is a glass ceiling for women everywhere Sharia law is considered the source of civil law and of marital/family law, whether in constitutions or in legislation.

Thus, in Egypt it has been established, for example, that a man has to receive approval from his first wife before entering into a second marriage. This is, without doubt, a form of progress which makes polygamy more difficult. However, to completely forbid polygamy legally in all Arab countries would be unthinkable at the moment. Until now, Tunisia has been an exception among Arab countries, with its law requiring monogamy. Though Sharia law itself might allow a number of interpretations, including an interpretation requiring monogamy, because of almost unanimous agreement on the part of theologians, polygamy is allowed. Additionally, Mohammed's example (and his polygamy), as it is recorded in tradition, counts as binding and as a source of Sharia law. As long as Sharia law is a source of civil legislation, polygamy will not be able to be touched in countries shaped by Islam.

The relationship with peace and violence

Likewise, the question regarding the extent to which violence may be employed to defend Islam has much to do with the topic of Sharia law. It also relates to what has been an uncritical view on the part of theology toward Islamic history and Mohammed's position as a role model. As is known, Mohammed began his proclamation of Islam in Mecca around the year 610 A.D. In addition to the call to turn to Allah, the sole God, before the final judgment would befall the world, he above all preached ethical commands up to 622 A.D. In 622 he immigrated to Medina, and for the last ten years of his life, until 632 A.D., his role developed far beyond being only a herald of Islam. Mohammed became the lawgiver and military leader of the first Islamic community. In Medina he conducted a number of battles and military campaigns. Some of the battles were initiated against him, but he also initiated some battles himself; he led both in wars of defense and of offense. From the depictions found in the Koran, we learn about the Battles of Badr and the Battle of Uhud, about battles against the Bedouins and Meccans, and also about campaigns against the Jewish tribes. In the Koranic reports of these struggles, there are numerous calls made upon believing Muslims to participate. For instance, the Koran contains the famous "Sword Verse," which commands the killing of heathen (Sura 9:5). At various points, the Koran speaks of "jihad" or as a verb "jahada," which translates as "make efforts, to struggle along God's way" (e.g., Sura 66:9; Sura 9:41). The Koran also speaks of "qital," the killing of enemies. In texts of the Koran which report battles or calls for conducting war, the terms *jihad* as well as *jahada* have almost exclusively a military meaning: they have to do with battling and killing along God's way (Sura 4:84; Sura 9:73).

Also, the idea that those killed in jihad will live (eternally) with God is a formula which is repeated in the Koran: "*think not of those who are slain in God's way as dead. Nay, they live . . . in the presence of their Lord; they rejoice in the bounty provided by God: And with regard to those left behind, who have not yet joined them (in their bliss), the (martyrs) glory in the fact that on them is no fear, nor have they (cause to) grieve*" (Sura 3:169-170).

Do these reports justify the exercise of violence today? Not necessarily. To begin with, these are reports of events occurring in the seventh century A.D. which require interpretation. In addition to the text of the Koran, there is the accompanying tradition (Arabic: hadith), which, to some extent, updates developments after Mohammed's death and includes the first generations of followers after Mohammed. In the eighth, ninth, and tenth centuries, tradition passed through a process of collection and sorting, which presumably came to a close in the tenth century. Tradition contains reports and directions on numerous topics, such as directions regarding fasting and prayer, on questions of everyday life, on marital and family law, on inheritance and criminal law, as well as on jihad. The tradition explains and expands much of which is only briefly depicted in the Koran. Thus, tradition also contains a number of reports and directions regarding battles along God's way and on thoughts relating to martyrdom, which frequently are linked to the prospects for paradise. These are also, first of all, historical reports which can be evaluated in very different ways. Islamic theology has set down numerous rules for jihad over the course of centuries, especially in the early days and during the time of expansion, but a foundational rejection of battle along God's way was never issued over the course of this history.

From the eighth century onward, we have found comprehensive compendia by Arab theologians and legal experts with respect to the ways and means of permitted and forbidden battle. However, there is no doctrinal position from the center of established theology which essentially declares jihad to be forbidden once and for all. There are definitely representatives who are of the opinion that jihad is solely allowed to be conducted with the tongue and hand, meaning that an individual is to say what is good and do what is good. Unfortunately, this has always remained a peripheral position, and this sort of teaching about peacemaking theology has not come from the center of established theology and institutes of learning. Naturally, this does not mean that most Muslims have started wars against their contemporaries. But when jihadists have invoked classical theologians and their interpretations, they cannot be easily refuted by pointing out that Islam has nothing to do with terror or by saying that jihadists are not Muslims. The reason is that whoever would like to take the instruction to fight out of the early days of Islam, or out of the inviolability of the role model of Mohammed, can do so without abusing the sources as they have been interpreted by a number of theologians over the centuries.

Religious freedom

In countries shaped by Islam, religious freedom is an additional explosive issue, in particular for converts, those who think differently, dissidents, atheists, and non-Muslim minorities. Those countries will only be able to solve these questions satisfactorily, according to international human rights standards, if either a far-reaching social secularization occurs, which appears improbable at the moment, or if Islamic theology distances itself from Sharia law.

There are various positions taken regarding the question of religious freedom among Islamic theologians: a minority of theologians has expressed itself bluntly by saying that for them religious freedom is exclusively the freedom to belong to the one true religion, or to turn to it, and that the death penalty has to be administered to Muslims who express doubts or criticism regarding Islam. For an additional minority of theologians, religious freedom applies to everyone, thus meaning the freedom to accept Islam or to turn from it, completely in the sense of the UN Declaration of Human Rights. A "moderate" majority of theologians defines religious freedom in the following way: Non-Muslims – in particular Jews and Christians – living in countries shaped by Islam may keep their religion and do not have to convert to Islam. For Muslims, however, religious freedom exclusively means freedom of thought with the possibility of secretly harboring doubts about Islam. Whoever propagates his diverging notions is, according to the opinion of a broad majority of traditionally trained theologians, guilty of crimes which are worthy of death according to Sharia law. This is the case even if there are only a few countries in which it would be possible to bring an apostate before a court. Certainly, an apostate is quickly viewed by the society as an enemy of the state. It can sometimes be very dangerous when legal scholars in mosques call for the killing of apostates and then society persecutes such apostates or, in some cases, executes them in street killings. For instance, there is the case of the Egyptian secularist Farag Fawda, who was killed in a street killing in Cairo in 1992 after a fatwa (legal opinion) from al-Azhar University declared the execution of an apostate to be a legally valid act. Two scholars at al-Azhar University, Muhammad al-Ghazali and Muhammad Mazru'a, had convinced the later culprits that it was the religious duty of every believer to execute apostates.[28] The roots of this notion lie in Sharia law, which distinguished theologians essentially set down by the tenth century A.D. According to accepted Sunni and Shiite understandings, Sharia law calls for the administration of the death penalty for an apostate. For that reason, many Muslims, including representatives of classical Islamic theology, consider conversion to Islam on the part of an individual to be desirable and simultaneously condemn apostasy from Islam. This applies all the more if the "apostate" converts to another religion, for instance to the Christian faith, which is regarded as superseded and falsified. For that reason, Muslims who become Christians or, in a few cases, Buddhists, or join a non-recognized minority, such as the Baha'i, are confronted with ostracism, discrimination, or even persecution.

Consequences of apostasy from Islam

Families of converts often demonstrate a complete lack of understanding when it comes to a change of faith, and they frequently attempt to change converts' minds and sometimes threaten them. This is because, as a rule, apostasy means shame, treason, and outrage for the family. Indeed, an apostate cannot be condemned to death by law in most countries shaped by Islam, but, at the very least, an apostate can be disinherited. Divorce can be imposed upon an apostate since, according to the civil law of Arab states shaped by Sharia law, no Muslim female is allowed to be married to a non-Muslim man. Additionally, since according to Sharia law Muslim children are not allowed to be raised by a non-Muslim, an apostate is threatened with the withdrawal of his children. He often loses his job since there is hardly anyone who would employ a convert, and he often loses his home. It is often the case that he is cast out of his family. In dramatic cases, it can go so far that members of the family or society lay their own hands on the convert and mistreat him, force him to be committed to psychiatric care, or even attempt to kill him. Some believe that the public loss of face by having a convert in one's family cannot be tolerated, while others hear from an imam or a mullah that, according to Sharia law, it is the duty of every believer to kill converts without any court hearings. Some are convinced that Islam is being defended when an apostate is killed, since, it is claimed, the Western world – in particular, the USA – has set out to destroy Islam and bribes people to convert in order to send them out as spies.

---

[28] See, for instance, the portrayal of the case in Armin Hasemann, "Zur Apostasiediskussion im Modernen Ägypten," in *Die Welt des Islam* 42/1 (2002), pp. 72-121.

Owing to the fact that religiously determined civil law makes it presently impossible to leave Islam in all Arab countries, as far as Sharia law is concerned, children of apostates are forced to remain Muslim. They have to be raised as Muslims, meaning that they have to attend Islamic religious instruction. They can only enter into an Islamic marriage, and their children likewise count legally as Muslims even if they, their parents, and grandparents were converts to Christianity. In a number of states, a converted married couple or a parent who has converted find themselves in danger of losing their children if, for instance, a relative files a formal legal complaint claiming that "Muslim children" are not allowed to grow up with Christians, which Sharia law forbids. For that reason, in Muslim majority countries the charge of unbelief and blasphemy count among the most serious charges of all. The charge is not only raised when a person leaves Islam or is guilty of blasphemy. Sometimes it is also directed against unpopular political opponents or is used to extort possessions. This is especially the case in Pakistan. Blasphemy laws have stood in Pakistan since colonial times and have been tightened step by step from 1980 onward, above all in order to exert pressure on the special Islamic community called the Ahmadiyya, though this tighter application of these laws is pressuring Christians as well.

Reasons for rejecting religious conversion

The most prominent statement in the Koran with respect to religious freedom is certainly the verse: "Let there be no compulsion in religion ..." (Sura 2:256). Numerous Islamic theologians have emphasized that no one can be forced to convert to Islam. This is at least reflected in parts of the history of Islamic conquest: Christians and Jews were generally allowed to retain their beliefs and their religious autonomy. Thus, they did not have to convert, but they were made "wards" (dhimmi), who were subject to special taxes and had to submit themselves. They were tolerated as second-class citizens, and thus they were the objects of legally enforced discrimination. This was because they were adherents of a religion which had been surpassed by Islam and which – owing to divergence from Islam – was said to be falsified. However, whoever had converted to Islam was not allowed to leave it. According to the predominant opinion of theologians, Sura 2:256 does not mean that Islam advocates free religious conversion in both directions and the legal equality of all religions. Instead, it is often interpreted that one cannot force any person into the act of "belief" (in the sense of a state of conviction). Given the fact that the Koran views Judaism and Christianity as inferior religions, there is a reason why conversion to Christianity is seen as essentially wrong: It appears to be a step backward to a religion which has been superseded. From the viewpoint of Islam, Christianity has been corrected by Islam and was supplanted by Mohammed, "the Seal of the prophets" (Sura 33:40). In Article 10 of the Cairo Declaration on Human Rights, Islam is mentioned as *"the religion of true unspoiled nature,"* thus the genuine religion which is naturally adequate for every person; every deviation from this counts as inferior. Additionally, Christianity is, for many theologians, a "Western" religion, a religion of crusades and colonial lords, which is thus linked to Western political domination.

A further reason for the rejection of freedom of religious conversion lies in the fact that turning away from Islam is not viewed by many Muslims as a private affair. Rather, it is a disgrace for the entire family or is even viewed as a political act, as a civil disturbance, as unrest, or even as a declaration of war on the Muslim community. This perception of conversion from Islam is rooted in early Muslim history. After Mohammed's death in 632 A.D. there were a number of tribes on the Arabian Peninsula which had accepted Islam but had then turned from it. Abu Bakr, the first Caliph after Mohammed, fought these tribes in the so-called Ridda Wars (Wars of Apostasy) and successfully defeated the uprising. Owing to these violent uprisings at the time of early Islam, apostasy is still linked in the collective consciousness of the Muslim community with political unrest, with treason, and with the violent conquest of this treason.

Dealing with apostates

On the one hand, the Koran itself speaks about unbelief on the part of people and of those who "strayed" (Sura 2:108) and threatens that apostates will "land in Hell" (Sura 4:115); but on the other hand, it does not define an earthly punishment and mentions no procedure for flawlessly determining the state of apostasy. A number of verses even appear to suggest the free choice of religion (e.g., Sura 3:20), while others, for instance Sura 4:88-89, enjoin Muslims to *"seize them and slay them"* if they *"turn renegades."* Thus, one confronts ambiguous findings when it comes to the texts. They are construed by a number of Muslim theologians in a way that says the Koran fully advocates religious freedom since, with respect to the state of affairs of apostasy, there is no unequivocal textual finding which can be put forth. Others, however, argue that the Koran establishes the death penalty for apostasy, for example, owing to verses such as Sura 4:88-89. Here one finds first of all that there is talk of *"hypocrites"* who wish that everyone was as unbelieving as they are. Then one reads: *"But take not friends from their ranks until they flee In the way of God (from what is forbidden). But if they turn renegades, seize them and slay them wherever ye find them; and (in any case) take no friends or helpers from their ranks."* Sura 9:11-12 also concerns those who have become adherents of the Muslim community (verse 11 mentions remorse, ritualistic prayer, and the giving of alms as characteristics of their new affiliation to Islam), but then they *"violate their oaths."* There is a call to *"fight ye the chiefs of unfaith."* There are a number of theologians who derive political imperilment of the Muslim community by apostates from these verses, as well as from the Ridda Wars (the violent defeat of movements which fell away after Mohammed's death).

Islamic tradition, which was compiled up to the ninth and tenth centuries (with reports about Mohammed and the first Muslims and their actions), far more sharply condemns turning away and also calls more clearly for the death penalty. Tradition expressly utilizes the term "apostasy" for turning away from Islam and reports on the execution of individual apostates, for instance, by the caliphs, and repeatedly calls for administering the death penalty to apostates. In this context, the most frequently quoted tradition is a quotation traceable back to Mohammed: *"Whoever changes his Islamic religion, then kill him."* Other theologians, in turn, doubt the authenticity of this saying and do not allow it as justification for the death penalty. Admittedly, up to the tenth century, one finds that the founders and students of the four schools of Sunni legal thought, as well as those of the most significant Shiite school, fully supported this call for administering the death penalty for turning away from Islam. The result has been that the majority of influential theologians from the early days of Islam call for the death penalty in the case of conversion and set this down in a binding manner in the penal code texts in Sharia compendia.

The fact is that from the early days of Islam onward, and throughout the entirety of Islamic history, people have been executed because of turning away from Islam. Likewise, there have also been cases of pardon transmitted through tradition. Whether the death penalty, particularly in the early days of Islam, was administered in every case, or whether the apostate received the opportunity to express remorse, as well as who was justified to judge in cases of apostasy, are all things which cannot be seamlessly reconstructed from history.

Apostasy in the twentieth century

The discussion of apostasy took a completely new turn in the twentieth century. In connection with the emergence of Islamism (the new varieties of radical Islam), and the call for political-Islamic powers to apply Sharia law to its full extent, there have been increased calls for the execution of apostates. Progressive interpreters of the Koran, women's rights activists, critical journalists and authors, secularists, along with members of minority groups are increasingly being charged with apostasy. As a result, in the final ten years of the twentieth century, there were at least 50 charges of apostasy brought to court in Egypt. Among these incidents is the famous case of the Koran scholar Nasr Hamid Abu Zayd, who had to flee from Egypt to the Netherlands in 1996 owing to charges of apostasy. At that time, a number of theologians even called for the introduction of the death penalty in Egyptian law. In particular, Islamists endeavor to increasingly point to the early days of Islam in order to show that the prosecution of apostates "has always" been practiced, and, besides that, "in Islam" it is a mandatory course of action since the case of apostasy is an issue of a capital offense. Apostasy in modern times is frequently equated with treason, insurgency, a revocation of political loyalty, and revolution.

The majority of classic Islamic theologians might endorse the opinion of the internationally influential Egyptian scholar Yusuf al-Qaradawi (b. 1926). According to him, a Muslim may harbor doubts within himself, and of course the deepest recesses of an individual are not accessible to anyone and therefore cannot be judged. But, according to al-Qaradawi's point of view, the individual is not allowed to speak with anyone about his doubts, may not convert to another religion, and may not attempt to entice anyone away from Islam. He is also not allowed to criticize Sharia law, Islam, the Koran, or Mohammed in any way. If he does so, al-Qaradawi views this as bringing about upheaval, treason, and divisiveness within the Muslim community, and it has to be prevented and punished. Al-Qaradawi holds the administration of the death penalty to be compulsory in this case. His definition of "freedom of belief" does not mean religious freedom. Rather, it only means internal freedom of thought and freedom of conviction, without this being allowed to be expressed. For this reason, a personal confession becomes treason against the state.

In summary, what we have today is that even though the constitutions of a number of countries whose cultures are shaped by Islam recognize the right to religious freedom,[29] in practice there is not comprehensive, positive and negative religious freedom in all directions. Rather, there is only

---

[29]   For a number of examples from the corresponding passages from the constitutions of Syria, Jordan, Algeria, Yemen, Mauritania and Morocco, which guarantee religious freedom, see: Sami A. Aldeeb Abu-Sahlieh, "Le Délit d'Apostasie

the freedom to convert to Islam or to retain Islam. In the process, owing to the frequent dramatic consequences for the apostate, the question of religious freedom is not only a religious question. Rather, religious conversion also has social and political consequences. Even if many Muslims would personally never lay a hand on a convert or would at least see his condemnation as problematic, one has the following situation: since both classical and contemporary forms of Islamic theology have never put forth a widely accepted positive justification of religious freedom nor an essential condemnation of the death penalty for apostasy, a rapprochement between countries characterized by Islam and religious freedom has been prevented. In addition, what has up to today been lacking is a general definition of apostasy, such that a very changeable understanding of the term could be applied to all sorts of situations. Thus, the question must be asked if Egypt and the remaining countries of the MENA region will decide for equal coexistence between religious communities and can find justifications which are acceptable in their societies. Alternatively, the question is whether religious freedom decisions will continue to be made from an orientation toward Sharia law – or an even stricter orientation toward Sharia law – which, at the minimum, discriminates against atheists and minorities, converts, and dissidents, and even threatens them in their very existence.

The position of non-Muslims in countries characterized by Islam

Which rights minorities will have in the future in the MENA region will also decide whether the region will develop in the direction of democracy. The ultimate question is: who will define the civil rights and liberties of the minorities? Will it be Sharia law or secular law (with the latter assuming a separation between religion and politics and the principle of equal treatment for all religious groups)?

Prior to the emergence of Islam, Jews and Christians, who are now living as minorities in the Middle East and in Northern Africa, made up the majority of the population in most of the countries. Over the centuries, the situation reversed. The reasons were wars of conquest, internal theological disputes within the church – for example, regarding the nature of Christ – power politics and nepotism, the prohibition against conversion from Islam to Judaism or Christianity, opportunities for advancement after

---

aujourd'hui et ses Conséquences en Droit Arabe et Musulman," in *Islamochristiania* (20) 1994, pp. 93-116, here pp. 96ff.

conversion to Islam, inheritance regulations which favored conversion to Islam, and marital laws which saw to it that children of mixed marriages were raised as Muslims. At the same time, there was also a policy of tolerance which made the reign of Islamic conquerors appear more bearable in parts then under Byzantine reign. Nowadays, Judaism has become a dwindling minority in the Middle East and Northern Africa. In a number of countries in which there used to be a large Jewish community, such as Yemen, Judaism has completely disappeared. Christianity also accounts for a numerically small minority in Northern Africa and the Middle East. In a number of regions, such as Saudi Arabia or Yemen, which had large Christian communities before the emergence of Islam, there are today no officially recognized indigenous Christians or churches.

Overall, the established Evangelical, Catholic, and Orthodox churches in the region have registered declines, while, simultaneously, the number of newly founded independent Christian house churches is steadily increasing in some countries. Due to the pressure of persecution, the new house churches are often underground. A number of these house churches (e.g., in Morocco) are silently tolerated, while others (e.g., in Iran) meet at the risk of their lives. Owing to this development, there are more than a few experts who are asking the question – and this all the more in the face of the massive refugee movements of Christians, such as those from Iraq, in recent years – whether Christianity will share the destiny of Judaism, with the imminent extinction of traditional Christian churches in this region. Such a development appears to be absolutely conceivable. Egypt constitutes an exception with its relatively large Christian minority of approximately eight-to-twelve million Coptic Christians.

Jews and Christians, however, are not the sole minorities in societies characterized by Islam in Northern African and the Middle East. In addition to Jewish and Christian groups, there are minority groups which have come forth from Islam or which unite Islamic, Gnostic, and Christian elements and are largely condemned as heretics by traditional Islamic theology. In some places they are politically threatened (e.g., the Baha'i in Egypt), while in other places, in spite of public condemnation, they are tolerated (e.g., Sunnis in Iran) or bitterly persecuted as "blasphemers" (e.g., the Ahmadiyya movement in Pakistan). A number of minorities do not solicit for their faith. Rather, they consist exclusively of members who are born into their community (e.g., the Druse community in Lebanon), while others are identical with ethnic groups in the form of national churches (e.g., Assyrians or Armenians). In the case of others, their status – as an Islamic minority or as their own religious community – has not been conclusively settled (e.g., in the case of the Alevites in Turkey).

The relationship to non-Islamic minorities in societies characterized by Islam in Northern Africa and the Middle East is predominantly defined by three factors: history, whereby the person of Mohammed is seen as exemplary; the statements in the Koran and tradition (Arabic: hadith) covering how to deal with non-Muslims; and Islamic law (above all, regulations covering minorities in Sharia law). In the societal realm, the relationship to minorities is determined by religiously shaped social norms, which are prescribed by influential theologians and institutions of learning. To be mentioned as leading the way in this area are al-Azhar University in Egypt and influential theologians such as Yusuf al-Qaradawi (b. 1926), arguably the most renowned Sunni theologian. He is the author of some 120 books, operates three of his own websites, and has his own television program.

Sharia law and minorities

When Mohammed began to preach Islam on the Arabian Peninsula around 610 A.D., he primarily preached to the polytheistic Arab tribes but as well hoped for recognition among Jews and Christians. He initially judged Jews and Christians rather positively as "believing in God" and "having faith" (Sure 5:82; 3:110). He presented himself to them as the final prophet in history, who concluded the line of prophets following Abraham, Moses, and Jesus. When neither Jews nor Christians accepted his claim to having been sent (Sura 2:111; 5:15), Mohammed began to battle militarily against Jewish groups from 624 A.D. onward, after his relocation to Medina, and over the course of the years, he increasingly condemned Christians theologically. Finally, he mainly condemned Christians because of their teaching on the Trinity – from the Koran's viewpoint, the worship of "three gods": God, the Son, and the Mother of God – as "blasphemers" (Sura 2:116; 5:72-73). The teaching on the sinfulness of all people, their salvation through the death of Jesus on the cross (Sura 4:157-158), and Jesus' resurrection are also rejected by the Koran. At the end of his life, the Christian faith was regarded by Mohammed as distorted and superseded; later Islamic theology viewed the Christian faith in the same way. For that reason, Judaism and Christianity, as well as all other earlier religions, are seen as corrected and displaced by the Koran, which, from the Islamic point of view, is the sole reliable scripture, which was handed down by Islam, which, from this perspective, is the sole unadulterated primary religion or prototypical religion. This feeling of superiority toward all other religions on the part of Islamic theology has led to religions not mentioned in the Koran, and, above all, any religion coming after the Koran, being viewed as unbelief and idolatry, while in the Koran, one finds that Jews and Christians are "people of the book." Indeed, they are not completely "unbelievers," and they are not heathen, but they have the reputation of deliberately rejecting the justified claim that Mohammed was sent as a prophet. Furthermore, they are considered to hold to an inferior religion quasi against their better judgment, making themselves guilty of the charge of "polytheism" and, that said, making them guilty of the worst sin of all.

This understanding of the Koran and tradition, which is found in numerous theological treatments by influential scholars from the early days of Islam up to modern times, has consistently influenced the status of Jews and Christians in societies shaped by Islam. That means that, as a rule, Jews and Christians have a right to exist, but religiously and legally they do not count as "equals;" they are second-class citizens. But minority groups which arose after the Koran, and which are, therefore, non-recognized minorities, possess no legal status (e.g., the Baha'i religious community in Egypt), nor do converts from Islam to another religion. At the present time, the free exercise of religion and an equal status for Muslims, Jews, Christians, Baha'i, Buddhists, and possibly other religious groups do not exist in any country characterized by Islam which invokes Sharia law as a legal source.

On the basis of their being partially recognized in areas conquered by Islam after Mohammed's death, Jews and Christians became "protected persons" (Arabic: dhimmi), who, as a rule, were not placed before the choice of conversion or death. They were allowed to retain their religious affiliation, but they nevertheless remained subjects. They were second-class citizens: special taxes were levied and they were discriminated against. The legal literature from the early years of Islam and in the Middle Ages mentions numerous regulations which obligated Jews and Christians to be recognizable by everyone when they were in public, for example, by the clothes they wore. They were only to ride donkeys instead of horses, were always to yield to Muslims, were never to build their houses higher than those of Muslims, and many other things. These regulations humiliated them, limited them, and led them to feel the fact of their discriminated status on a daily basis. Nowadays, there is a broad consensus in research that Jews principally enjoyed a better status of legal protection in Islamic Middle Age societies than they did at the same time in European societies. This is the case even though we also know of examples of infringements on this legally defined status which occurred in countries characterized by Islam. At various times, Jews and Christians were able to rise in the service of their rulers and fill influential posts. At other times, there were pogroms and excesses against Jews and Christians. But there has not been a basic rejection of their minority-right status from the core of established Muslim theology to the present time. This is because established Muslim theologians have not allowed a disengagement from the interpretive pattern of Sharia law of early Islam and of the role model of Mohammed. This is reflected in the discriminated status of minorities in societies characterized by Islam to the present day.

The current situation minorities face in societies characterized by Islam

The framework for defining the legal status of minorities in countries shaped by Islam continues to be oriented toward the guidelines of Sharia law. This is based upon the Koran, tradition (Arabic: hadith), and the development of law in the early days of Islam up to the tenth century. It is by that time that Sharia law counts as existing in its final formulation and set down in legal compendia for the broad majority of established theologians. These compendia are also considered to be binding to the present day. Within established theology at universities and mosques, Sharia law counts everywhere as God-given, perfect, and immutable in the regulations it contains, even if it is taught as interpretable law when applied. On the one hand, Sharia law is only partially applied in a large share of countries characterized by Islam, above all, in civil law. Thus, Sharia law is applied in estate law, marital law, and family law. Sharia criminal law, on the other hand, does not apply in most countries. And yet, there is the theoretical claim that has been perpetuated in an uninterrupted fashion and thus affects minorities' legal and social positions. For that reason, it is impossible for Jews and Christians to enjoy the same rights as Muslims in a state where Sharia law is invoked as a source of law. There are countries where Sharia law is applied in civil and criminal law (e.g., in Iran), and in other countries Sharia law is applied in part (above all, in issues relating to civil law – in Egypt, for example). Still in others, Sharia law is completely invalid (such as is the case in Turkey). However, true freedom of choice in issues relating to religion exists nowhere in Arab countries.

In the course of contemporary developments – the so-called Arabellion – religious minorities, including converts in Northern Africa and the Middle East, become increasingly entangled between the fronts of secularists and, above all, Islamists, who have in part spoken out for additional legal discrimination against minorities. Even if they have suffered under various legal restrictions over the past decades, at least their status as a minority was "protected" to a certain extent. This was the case for acknowledged, traditional Christian minorities, such as the members of Catholic, Orthodox, and Protestant churches. Governments in Arab countries have, till now, rarely generated active persecution of religious minorities and special groups, even if they have offered too little protection from attacks against minorities. Governments have not consistently prosecuted offenders, have legally discriminated against minorities, and have not eliminated social discrimination against minorities. It is feared that this could fundamentally change under governments shaped by political Islam. There are already exceptions to this "policy of tolerance," found particularly in Iran and Saudi Arabia.

Wherever Sharia law possesses validity with respect to civil law in Arab countries, marriages between Muslim women and Christian or Jewish men are essentially prohibited. In those locations, anyone born into a Muslim family may not leave Islam and may not change his profession of faith. His entry in the birth registry as a Muslim may, under no circumstances, be removed. In a country with civil law shaped by Sharia law, a non-Muslim cannot inherit anything from Muslim relatives. There, a convert to Christianity can be forced to divorce by court decree, and his children can be taken from him and handed over to a Muslim family. According to the same law, a 17-year old young man automatically becomes a Muslim if his Christian father converts to Islam. From this time onward, he must take Islamic religious instruction and may only enter into an Islamic marriage. A Muslim man may essentially – except in Tunisia and Turkey – enter into a polygamous marriage and cannot be legally hindered by anyone. A woman essentially inherits only one-half of the portion of an inheritance and is, according to Sharia law, highly restricted in the possibilities she has to divorce.

E. Why are human rights improvements so difficult to achieve?

Why then does it appear to be so difficult to bring about undisputed improvements in the human rights situation in countries characterized by Islam, even though the majority of people seem to desire greater freedoms? It is undesirable political developments, economic underdevelopment, a high percentage of illiteracy, and overall a largely lacking civil society are preventing successful political participation. However, as much as undesirable economic, social, and political developments play a role, what cannot be overlooked is the fact that one of the difficulties in this connection remains the constriction on human rights within the framework of Sharia law. Sharia law is largely proclaimed in an uncritical manner and promulgated as the eternally valid law of God from lecterns at universities and from pulpits at mosques. Given its traditional a-historic interpretation at universities and mosques, Sharia law is divested of any criticism and is considered to be the standard for life in the here and now. It is also viewed as the standard for the definition of human rights. As long as that remains the case, liberal or secular justifications of comprehensive human rights can only be established at the margins of society and frequently with risks for the critics of the current situation: "*A number of Muslim reform theologians see an opportunity to overcome certain traditions with human rights standards. ... And yet, their political influence is comparatively small.*"[30] If, for instance, democracy only appears conceivable if it can be discovered in the Koran with Mohammed and his fellow companions, a secular justification of democracy is hardly imaginable; this is also true if whatever type of majority cannot discover this prototypical form of democracy in Mohammed.

Even if Sharia law is, for the most part, only applied in civil law matters in Arab countries, the practical meaning of the Sharia is not to be underestimated. The norms of Sharia law are present in everyday life through sermons held in mosques; through texts from tradition quoted at weddings, funerals, and similar events; through traditions and the sense of justice present in many fields: "*many Arab countries...[are] permeated by Sharia law handed down in a manner which is elusive in its reconstruction ... such that all Muslims subject to it have their actions and expressions of life first and foremost delineated before God in gradated forms of what is allowed and what is objectionable. It is the religious law of Sharia law which regulates the collective and individual convictions and behavioral expectations in what is a measure that is difficult to reconstruct for a Western academic's analytical grasp. They are not uncoupled from Sharia law, for instance, as a tangible area of norms for law and morality or of simply a 'reasonable' set of ethics, which is characteristic for the more or less positivistic legal order in the realm of continental Europe with its separation of religion and law and of politics and morality.*"[31]

What is stronger than the influence of Sharia law on legislation is its social impact, because a large part of the population would place neither the infallibility of the text of the Koran into question nor the essential assessment of Sharia law as an indispensable divine norm. Therefore, the

---

[30]   Ali al-Nasani, "Menschenrechte im Islam," amnesty international 01/2002, http://www.amnesty.de/umleitung/2002/deu05/010?lang=de%26mime-type%3dtext%2fhtml (accessed December 18, 2012).

[31]   Birgit Krawietz, *Die Hurma: Schariarechtlicher Schutz vor Eingriffen in die körperliche Unversehrtheit nach arabischen Fatwas des 20. Jahrhunderts* (Berlin: Duncker & Humblot, 1991), p. 77.

justification of Sharia law for configuring a way of life – at least in theory – also remains unquestioned. Sharia norms are conveyed via Koran schools, sermons given in mosques, reports found in tradition, fatawa (legal opinions), literature, the internet, discussion circles, and scholarly circles. These norms produce a general legal consciousness which, at least in an emotional sense, is more strongly oriented toward the norms of Sharia law than is the official theology found within universities. These norms shape popular opinion more than the moderate orientation of certain countries would lead one to assume. And in an environment with this general consciousness, Sharia norms are essentially non-negotiable. Rather, they are, at most, a matter of interpretation.

F. Preconditions for the development of "Islamic democracies"

It is not to be expected that there will be a foundational and comprehensive improvement in the human rights situation and in the development of true, stable democracies in countries characterized by Islam as long as the theoretical claim of Sharia law is not allowed to be placed under review by official representatives of Islamic theology. As Bassam Tibi has formulated it: "That means that without a radical reform of religion and law in Islam, which, for example, the Sudanese lawyer Abdullahi An-Na'im endorses, there will not be a synthesis between Islam and human rights."[32] To leave the complete theoretical demands of Sharia law and its influential conservative and political interpretation untouched means, however, to assign critics of Sharia law to exile or to anonymity. And if Sharia norms remain significantly untouched in their claims, the framework for their interpretation will naturally remain very limited and their practical expansion *de facto* extremely difficult. As long as an imitation of seventh-century Arabian Society is viewed by theological and even influential political institutions as synonymous with justice, progress, and true civilization, critical contention with the claims of Sharia law can hardly be expected. *"From the point of view of religion, modernity appears to be a demonstration of a loss and backsliding since it has left its true origins and premises behind."*[33]

---

[32] Bassam Tibi, *Im Schatten Allahs: Der Islam und die Menschenrechte* (München: Piper, 1996), p. 45.

[33] Adonis, "Die Sackgasse der Moderne in der arabischen Gesellschaft," in Erdmute Heller and Hassouna Mosbahi (eds.), *Islam, Demokratie, Moderne: Aktuelle Antworten arabischer Denker* (München: C. H. Beck, 1998), pp. 62-71, here p. 69.

Some still hope that official theology will open up to a historical critical treatment of Sharia law in the foreseeable future. For that reason it must be stated that a fundamental precondition for the development of true democracies in societies characterized by Islam would be a restriction of Islam to the area of ritual religious exercise and personal morality, with a simultaneous rejection of Sharia law as the shaping component of the legal system, as well as of the political and social orders, in particular with respect to women's rights, human rights, minority rights, the freedom of religion, and civil liberties. Democracy does not only mean holding elections. Elections, even if they have been sham elections, have been held in most Arab countries. Rather, democracy also means responsibility on the part of the individual, a constitutional state, independent courts, legal equality and equal opportunity, tolerance toward those who think differently, the freedom of opinion, as well as the right to openly confess oneself to be an atheist. If these rights are to be affirmed and justified, and if majorities are to be found for the endorsement of these rights, it will only be possible when a reformation of theology occurs. What continues to rule in the realm of institutional theology and established theologians is the notion that Islam is not only a religion but also a sociopolitical order.

III. Current positions of Muslim intellectuals regarding democracy

There are in effect three positions on democracy held by Muslim theologians and intellectuals at present:

1. An attitude of complete rejection.
2. A superficial position of agreement which, however, replaces parts of democracy with Islamic principles and measures democracy against the standards of Islamic law.
3. A position of complete endorsement which, however, is limited to intellectuals, theologians, philosophers, journalists, and regime critics who neither have professorships at universities nor teach in large institutes of learning and mosques and have, in part, fled to Western countries for fear of their life and well-being.

A. Voices rejecting democracy

At the present time, clear voices of rejection respecting democracy come primarily from the realm of Islamism. Not only is criticism brought against democracy. At the same time, alternatives are brought forth for a state completely submitted to Sharia law.

Abu l-A'la Maududi

One of the most prominent Muslim theologians fundamentally rejecting democracy was Abu l-A'la Maududi (1903-1979), an intellectual, an ideologue, an author of over 130 works, the writer of an influential commentary on the Koran, a political activist, and an advisor to several Pakistani government administrations. With his writings on "theo-democracy" and the "rule of God," he exercised significant influence on the most important leaders of Arab and Iranian Islamism, such as Sayyid Qutb and Ruhollah Khomeini. Maududi counts as one of the most prominent masterminds of statehood founded upon an Islamic foundation, a foundation which rests solely upon the rule of God and rejects any man-made responsibility for control of the state. Among the most important thoughts he formulated with respect to the founding of this Islamic political system is the unconditional emphasis on the sovereignty and reign of God (Arabic: hakimiyat

Allah), which is for Maududi the sole legitimate rule and which is placed over every dominion on earth. It obligates every government to act as God's representative, to bring all existing laws into agreement with Sharia law, to abolish all other laws, and to base the administration of justice exclusively upon Sharia law. According to Maududi, people should ideally be convinced to accept the introduction of Sharia legislation; if necessary, coercion may be used as a final means. This rule of God, which develops where rulers apply the law of God, i.e., Sharia law, has, from Maududi's point of view, wrongly been given up. Instead, other rulers, such as kings, have been put in God's place. Such rulers are usurpers, their rule is illegitimate, and acknowledgment of their rule is polytheism (thus, apostasy from Islam).

Maududi understood Islam as a holistic system leading an individual on the way of faith, on the way of a peaceful social order, as well as on the path of just state legislation. This legislation is to be taken from Sharia law so that through its complete implementation, a body politic superior to all other systems emerges on its own.[34] This holistic Islam will be implemented with the aid of an avant-garde of believing Muslims, at the head of which will be a male, Muslim, adult, spiritually healthy member of the Muslim community as a leader (Arabic: amir), the political head of state. He and his committee of advisors will be "elected." For that reason, according to Maududi, this state model is, ultimately, a democratic system which, however, does not apply human ordinances but rather brings about the application of God's laws. For that reason, Maududi calls his form of the state "theo-democracy" or a "democratic caliphate," since the top leadership will be elected from especially selected faithful individuals and receives the mandate through the people to Islamize the state completely. God – and not the people, as in Western democracies, which from Maududi's point of view means tyranny and despotism – possesses the highest sovereignty in this state. Because this state is an ideological state, only those who share this ideology have a right to be in positions of leadership or influence. An advisory council, to which neither women nor non-Muslims may belong, will advise the ruler, who theoretically can be overthrown in the case of deviation from Sharia law. He should distinguish himself through his piety and good moral behavior, although Maududi always remains vague in his writings about what that concretely means. All

---

[34]   See in part regarding Maududi's political ethics, S. Abu A'la Mawdudi, *The Islamic Law and Constitution* (Lahore: Islamic Publications Ltd., 1955/1980[7]), pp. 123ff.

people in this system are, without exception, "vice-regents," thus representatives or God's caliphs[35], who elect the avant-garde of the elite and only differ from each other in their character or in their abilities but are otherwise completely equal before God. Owing to their own complete implementation of Islam and submission to God, they ensure that the best representatives will be elected.

Such a society is, in Maududi's eyes, the realization of ideal community, in which neither injustice nor oppression, neither hate nor avarice exist, for through its faithfulness toward God, humankind overcomes its arrogance and keeps its egoism under control. Through absolute loyalty in allegiance to God, humankind becomes completely free and builds a "community of the center." Laws will not be made by people in this state since God has already given his perfect law, Sharia law, to humankind. Sharia law is only to be interpreted and brought to bear through analogy (through inference to parallel cases in the early days of Islam). Parties are unnecessary in this system since the political orientation is prescribed by the law of God. States which do not put this system into practice are, according Maududi's understanding, on the way to godlessness.

Maududi employs no thoughts regarding the question of how to respond to a misinterpretation of God's law by the highest ruler and his advisors and, respectively, how the correct interpretation and application of Sharia law within a sociopolitical framework is to be determined. Maududi assumed that personal integrity, faith and morality, the fear of God, and complete loyalty to God and his law would automatically prevent unauthorized and misguided action. Furthermore, he assumed that in such a state under the order of Sharia law, peace and unity would develop by themselves, for people's membership in (true) Islam, their obedience, and their submission would cause all differences and discrepancies to disappear: Islam is politics, politics is the implementation of ethics and morality,[36] and citizenship is membership in the community of Muslims (umma). With this, Maududi proclaimed that piety is the healing means for all social problems. With a complete implementation of Islam, social problems would come to a halt.

---

[35] Maududi explains this farther. See S. Abul A'la Maududi, *Ethical Viewpoint of Islam* (Lahore: Islamic Publications Ltd., 1966²/1967³), p. 26.

[36] For instance, see Maududi's remarks on the "Moral System of Islam" in his work, Sayyid Abul A'la Maududi, *Islamic Way of Life* (Lahore: Islamic Publications Ltd., 1950/1965³/1986), pp. 31ff.

Sayyid Qutb

In a similar fashion, Sayyid Qutb (1906-1966), who had been influenced by Maududi, the *spiritus rector* of the Egyptian Muslim Brotherhood, expressed his thinking in his programmatic essay "Milestones upon the Way." It is one of the most influential publications of political Islam ever to have been produced. Qutb desires *"the establishment of the sovereignty of God and His Lordship throughout the world, the end of man's arrogance and selfishness, and the implementation of the rule of divine Shari'ah in human affairs."*[37] For according to his estimation, *"Mankind today is on the brink of a precipice, not because of the danger of complete annihilation which is hanging over its head – this being just a symptom and not the real disease – but because humanity is devoid of those vital values which are necessary not only for its healthy development but also for its real progress."*[38] For that reason, according to Qutb's understanding, Muslims may only accept the Sharia as law, which he considered to be a panacea against every ill of civilization, and nothing else: *"The basis of the message is that one should accept Shari'ah law without any question and reject all other laws in any shape or form. This is Islam. There is no other meaning of Islam."*[39]

Today there are also some voices, above all on the internet, generally following the reasoning of Qutb and Maududi, which prevent Muslims in Western countries from voting or from acknowledging democracy, for from this point of view, *"democracy is a man-made system, meaning rule by the people for the people. Thus it is contrary to Islam, because rule is for Allah, the Most High, the Almighty, and it is not permissible to give legislative rights to any human being, no matter who he is."*[40]

B.   A partial approval of democracy

For all intents and purposes, those who do not reject democracy head-on but rather want to co-opt it for Islam and thus, in the final event, Islamize it, do not truly want to accept democracy. They want to use it for their own purposes, with the goal of being able to recast it over the long term. Ostensibly, democracy is affirmed by many representatives of political Islam (Islamism). As a general rule, they endorse "acknowledging" democracy.

---

[37]   Shahid Shaykh Sayyid Qutb, *Ma'alim fi t-tariq. Zeichen auf dem Weg* (Köln: Al-Azr/M. Rassoul, 2005), pp. 70-71, quoted from: http://www.izharudeen.com/uploads/4/1/2/2/4122615/milestones_www.izharudeen.com.pdf (17.08.015).

[38]   Ibid., p. 11.

[39]   Ibid., p. 44.

[40]   http://islam-qa.com/en/ref/107166 (accessed November 5, 2012).

However, as long as they do not fundamentally reject the principle validity of Sharia-defined limitations on women's rights and minority rights, limited religious freedom, and the basic justification of an Islamic penal code (with corporal punishment), the assertion of a general "compatibility" between democracy and Sharia law is to be treated with caution.

Yusuf al-Qaradawi

Yusuf al-Qaradawi is an Islamic theologian who was born in Egypt in 1926 and has lived for over 50 years in exile in Qatar. Today he is perhaps the most famous Islamic theologian and is highly influential as an opinion leader. He has published around 120 books, innumerable fatwas (legal opinions), articles, and sermons, and he is the chairman of several umbrella organizations for Muslim scholars in Europe. He regularly appears on television programs broadcast by the Qatar station al-Jazeera. Today he counts as one of the most important representatives of Islamic "minority rights," which avails itself of democracy but does not want fundamentally to accept democracy. Thus, al-Qaradawi only wants to use the advantages of democracy for the propagation of Islam. As a representative of Islamic minority rights, al-Qaradawi claims Muslims may or should be allowed, for a time, to adapt to the laws in Europe while living in a diaspora situation. For the period of transition until Sharia law is introduced in its entirety, Muslims temporarily do not have to follow all the commands of Islam. This conception of law, which was discussed by Islamic theologians at the beginning of the 1990s at international conferences,[41] is based on two foundational assumptions:

1. Islam is a global religion, which justifies permanently remaining in the "diaspora."
2. The search for practical solutions according to the intentions of Islamic law is justified.

Owing to this, one is allowed to interpret Sharia law in a manner corresponding to life's requirements in non-Islamic societies. Also, in individual cases, one is allowed to offer forms of relief where the application of Sharia law is currently not possible. In this way, it should be possible for Muslims in non-Muslim countries to choose alternative solutions which are the best for them in the diaspora, if strictly following Sharia law is made impossible

---

[41]   Sarah Albrecht, *Islamisches Minderheitenrecht: Yusuf al-Qaradawis Konzept des fiqh al-aqalliyat* (Würzburg: Ergon, 2010), pp. 19f.

through the laws of these countries. According to al-Qaradawi, among the preconditions of this understanding is the Muslim minority becoming aware of its special identity and recognizing its task of recasting non-Islamic society into one which is Islamic. For that reason, from al-Qaradawi's point of view, Muslims in the diaspora may never essentially give up Sharia law as God's law, as it is in al-Qaradawi's eyes. Instead, they should be instructed in the commands of Islam, grow to become an elite in their societies, and through their example and their proclamation of Islam (Arabic: da'wa) seek to permeate the society with Sharia law.[42]

The goal of this type of minority right is not the integration of Muslim immigrants into European societies. Instead, in an inverse sense it obligates Muslims to live in European society as the permanent others and to tune into Qaradawi's programs on television and call up his fatwas and publications on the internet. They should indeed accept the European constitutional state but they should not ultimately acknowledge its legal authority. Rather, through education and the complete implementation of Islam, they should prepare for the coming time, in which things will have changed so much that the Muslim community's avant-garde, which will have been educated and trained in holistic Islam, can take over leadership.

It is therefore not surprising that al-Qaradawi, who advocates the complete application of Sharia legislation, including the administration of corporal punishment, also affirms the death penalty as the punishment for openly confessing converts and for those who are religionless, recommends husbands to chastise their disobedient wives, calls for suicide attacks on Israel, and does not envisage equal rights for women and non-Muslims. In many places where he has published his official statements in English, he does not defend these positions in a bold manner. Rather, he tends to soften and euphemize, while his (hardly read in Europe) writings composed in Arabic enumerate the mentioned points much more explicitly.[43]

As far as the effect of such prominent opinion makers is concerned, one should not have illusions: Never was the effect greater than today in the age of the internet. If a number of studies conducted independently of each other over many years show that between 45% and 49% of all Muslims in

---

[42]   Yusuf al-Qaradawi turns his attention to the special situation of Islamic minorities in non-Islamic societies in articles, fatawas, and in his work *fi fiqh al-aqalliyat al-muslima. hayat al-muslimin wasat al-mujtama'at al-uhra* (Cairo: Dar ash-shuruq, 2001).

[43]   For instance, compare the German edition of his work, Jusuf al-Qaradawi, *Erlaubtes und Verbotenes im Islam* (München: SKD Bavaria, 1989), at this point with the Arabic original: *al-halal wa-'l-haram fi 'l-islam* (Cairo: Dar ihya' al-kutub al-arabiya, 1960).

Germany see a conflict between Islam and democracy such that *"following the commands of my religion ... [is] more important to me than democracy,"*[44] then the influence of such voices of warning can be traced back to not becoming involved in Western society because it is "un-Islamic."

But how does one get to this high number of almost 50%? These Muslims are not to be counted among extremists or even as terrorists. However, they are influenced by Islamist opinion leaders such as al-Qaradawi: What is conveyed to them by scholars who are steeped in tradition and who are in part Islamist-oriented is that they have to decide between a fully implemented faith and the enemy camp. If they defend a more moderate Islam and affirm democracy with its civil rights and liberties, they are condemned by scholars such as al-Qaradawi as traitors of Islam. With this, al-Qaradawi Islamizes Western democracies by authoritatively expounding which elements of democracy are to be rejected and which can be accepted. At no point does he distance himself from the Sharia's claim to authority. Sharia law remains indispensable in Europe, as it is in the Middle East. In the process, al-Qaradawi is neither a Jihadist nor an extreme outsider. Rather, he is a theologian who was educated in a traditional manner at al-Azhar University in Cairo. He appears on television programs, on the internet, and in his publications with the habits, the language, and the typical clothing of a scholar and counts today as the authority of Sunni Islam. At the same time, he consistently places the choice of supporting the full practice of Sharia law or of betraying Islam before his listeners and viewers. In the best case, this message leads people who follow it into a parallel society. In the worst case, it leads them into a radicalism that completely rejects and condemns Western society.

Murad Hofmann

The German lawyer and former diplomat Murad Hofmann, who converted to Islam, has claimed "that a fundamental concern of democracy, namely the securing of an ordered, systematic control of governments in order to prevent arbitrariness of all kinds, is a matter that is at its core an Islamic

---

[44] For instance, the study "Muslime in Deutschland" from 2007 established the following numbers: 46.7% "rather" or "completely" agree that "following the commands of my religion ... [is] more important for me than democracy." Katrin Brettfeld/Peter Wetzels, *Muslime in Deutschland. Eine Studie des Bundesinnenministeriums zu Integration, Integrationsbarrieren, Religion und Einstellungen zu Demokratie, Rechtsstaat und politisch-religiös motivierter Gewalt. Ergebnisse von Befragungen im Rahmen einer multizentrischen Studie in städtischen Lebensräumen* (Hamburg: Universität Hamburg, 2007), p. 141.

concern."[45] But if that is the case, he has distorted the fundamental concern of democracy and placed it in the service of Islam. At the same time, he defends classic Islamist positions, such as the death penalty for apostates from Islam who "through refusal to pay taxes do damage [to Islam] or who stir up harm on earth,"[46] as legitimate and not as something which stands in fundamental conflict with human rights principles. According to Hofmann, where an Islamic head of state rules, Sharia law must be applied, legislation must orient itself toward Sharia law,[47] and Mohammed's political role model must followed.

Even if leading figures from within the Muslim community declare that terms such as "democracy" are completely compatible with Islam, they really create an Islamic form of democracy that is totally different from what is called democracy in the West. Ultimately, with regard to all considerations surrounding the unification of Islam and democracy, it is repeatedly a question of whether God or humanity is the source all legislation. Are people allowed to pass laws which, in cases of uncertainty, are in conflict with classical Sharia interpretations, or does the Islamic legal system have to be implemented in social and political realms today?

C. Affirming democracy

Over the past two decades, there have been a number of voices among Muslim intellectuals and theologians which have arisen and which deviate from the typical manner of argumentation of classical theologians. With the aid of various methods of textual interpretation, they have extracted justification for extended human rights, women's rights, and civil liberties. They have done this without confrontational opposition to the truth claims of the Koran. In Egypt and Iran in particular, there have been reformers who have come forth with alternative interpretations and concepts for defusing statements made in the Koran, in the tradition, and in Sharia law which discriminate against women and minorities. They foundationally reject corporal punishment and the death penalty in cases of falling away from the faith, and, respectively, argue that the application of corporal punishment and the death penalty is no longer compulsory.

---

[45]   Murad Hofmann, *Der Islam im 3. Jahrtausend: Eine Religion im Aufbruch* (Kreuzlingen: Diederichs, 2000), p. 116.

[46]   Ibid., pp. 99-100.

[47]   Murad Hofmann, *Der Islam als Alternative* (München: Diederichs, 1992), p. 77.

Mahmud Muhammad Taha

One of the most prominent representatives of this perspective is the founder of the Republican Brotherhood and reformed scholar Mahmud Muhammad Taha (b. 1909 or 1911). From his point of view, Islam was to be virtually equated with peace, equality between man and woman, democracy, and freedom. For him, the key to such an interpretation of Islam was found in taking Meccan (apolitical) early Islam from between the years of 610 A.D. and 622 A.D. as normative, not, however, the Medinan (political) or second epoch of Mohammed's life (622-632 A.D.). Medinan Islam is a type of "secular humanism,"[48] which he also labels as the "second message of Islam."[49] Of course, this has been a frontal attack on the advocates of the classical Sharia standpoint. For that reason, Taha, after a political power tug of war, was publicly executed at the advanced age of 75 in January 1985, shortly before the then Sudanese President Jafar Muhammad an-Numeiri was deposed. This has been one of the noticeably negative signals sent to the critical reform discussion within Islamic theology up to the present day.

Mohammad Shabestari

An additional pioneer in issues relating to human rights and civil liberties is the Iranian theologian, philosopher, reformer, and advocate of democracy, human rights, equality among religions, and freedom of opinion Mohammad Shabestari (b. 1936). He views human rights and democracy as quantities essentially contrived by people and about which the Koran makes no statements. For that reason, neither democracy nor human rights contradicts Islam. On the contrary, both are compatible with Islam as far as Shabestari is concerned. This is because they are products of reason and correspond to what Islam understands to be just rule. Additionally, democracy embodies an antidote against tyranny. Democracy and human rights are only a contemporary applications of principles of just rule on earth set down in the Koran.

Shabestari relativizes the timeless validity of the dominance held by Sharia regulations by, on the one hand, emphasizing the freedom of the

---

[48]   As formulated by Gereon Vogel, *Blasphemie: Die Affäre Rushdie in religionswissenschaftlicher Sicht; Zugleich ein Beitrag zum Begriff der Religion* (Frankfurt: Peter Lang, 1997), p. 30.

[49]   Compare Taha's own explanations in Mahmoud Mohamad Taha, *The Second Message of Islam*; translation and introduction by Abdullahi Ahmed an-Na'im (Syracuse: Syracuse University Press, 1987).

will of humanity and the necessity of voluntary faith. Shabestari sees "freedom and equality" manifested in democracy.[50] After that, he scrutinizes the ability of people to know absolute truth and relativizes any binding application of all the instructions in religious texts by concluding that they only applied in a literal sense at the time of their revelation. The "core of the divine message" applies eternally, not, however, its social implementation at that prior time.[51]

On the one hand, Shabestari's approach is indeed promising. On the other hand, however, he cannot remove the lack of a concrete justification for human rights, women's rights, and civil liberties from the texts of Islam. Additionally, such an approach cannot effectively suspend the directions in the Koran and tradition to fight against unbelievers and apostates or to discriminate against women. Indeed, Shabestari introduces hermeneutical principles of reason and a historicizing treatment of texts, but he neither explains the underlying supreme principle according to which one text is still completely valid while others are relegated to history, nor does he explain which texts belong to which category. With that said, he activates his own hermeneutic as a filter before the conventional understanding of the text – thereby, however, neither defusing the explosive nature of the passages which are not compatible with human rights nor having found a model of textual interpretation which will find a broad set of adherents.

Mohsen Kadivar

The Shiite cleric, philosopher, and writer Mohsen Kadivar (b. 1959) has likewise spoken out prominently on the topic of democracy.[52] As far as he is concerned, there are two ways of reading the Koran: one is the traditional form, which leads to trimming the rights of non-Muslims, women, and those who think differently; and the other is modern, in the direction of equality, religious freedom, and the freedom of opinion, an Islam with which democracy and freedom are possible. In the process, Kadivar goes so far as to assert that the incompatibility between Islam and democracy

---

50   Comp., for example, his text: Mohammad Mojtahed Shabestari, "Demokratie und Religiosität," in Katajun Amirpur, *Unterwegs zu einem anderen Islam: Texte iranischer Denker* (Freiburg: Herder, 2009), pp. 25-36, here p. 28.

51   Roman Seidel, Porträt Shabestari: "Glaube, Freiheit und Vernunft." http://de.qantara.de/Glaube-Freiheit-und-Vernunft/3240c3334i1p396/ (accessed December 18, 2012).

52   Numerous publications are found on his own home page: http://en.kadivar.com/ (accessed December 18, 2012).

and human rights lies not only in the interpretation of the Koran but is found in the wording of the Koran itself.

Kadivar breaks down the teaching of Islam into four areas. The first three are religious-ethical quantities, such as the belief in God and Mohammed, ethics, morality, and prayer. These areas are unalterable and valid for all times. The fourth area concerns the social and political regulations of Islam, such as women's rights, the penal code, individual rights, and the dress code. This fourth area is, in his opinion, alterable and must be adjusted in every era according to prevailing circumstances. Kadivar thus pleads for a historicizing of law and, in that manner, denies the traditional understanding of the Sharia's justification. Bahman Nirumand summarizes Kadivar's view as follows: *"How people regulate coexistence, and how they likewise configure politics, child-rearing, and education, how they take action against crimes and offenses – that is ruled by reason, prudence, experience, and science – on the basis of real life circumstances – which change permanently. This means, however, that in the final event Islamic legislation has to be rewritten and that politics has to be separated from religion."*[53]

Within the traditional interpretation of Islam and Sharia law, Kadivar recognizes no room for democracy and the equal rights of all people independent of their religion, gender, and their social position.[54] In this connection, he expresses himself particularly critically with respect to the disadvantaged position of women in countries whose cultures are shaped by Islam. He recognizes and mentions contradictions between certain statements made in the Koran and the Muslim tradition with human rights. For Kadivar, the solution lies in having certain provisions in their holy writings classified as only temporary. Kadivar belongs among the most courageous and foundational critics of the present-day balance of power in Iran and within traditional theology, which has earned him occasional imprisonment: in 1999, owing to his critical statements, he was sentenced to 18 months' imprisonment in Teheran's notorious Evin Prison. He has lived in exile in the United States since 2008.

---

[53] Bahman Nirumand, "Der iranische Reformer Mohsen Kadivar: Anpassung an zeitgemäße Lesarten des Islam," http://de.qantara.de/Anpassung-an-zeitgemaesse-Lesarten-des-Islam/849c812i1p97/ (accessed 18.12.2012).

[54] Ibid.

Abdolkarim Soroush

The Iranian intellectual and philosopher Abdolkarim Soroush (b. 1945) might be even better known than Shabestari.[55] Abdolkarim Soroush's actual name is Hossein Haj Farajullah Dabbagh. He is one of the most important representatives of the reform movement in Iran who argues religiously, not secularly, but still advocates human rights and civil liberties apart from the traditional understanding of Sharia law. Religion and its supreme truths are divine as far as Soroush is concerned. They are eternal and immutable. However, these eternal truths are not exactly what people generally believe they possess as religious knowledge and not what people generally interpret these truths to be. There are no absolute certainties for him. This is because God's law is in the final event unfathomable, and humankind's insights change. In no case can something which is inhuman or unreasonable be true, for that which is unreasonable does not correspond to God's will: *"It is reason that defines truth."*[56]

In Soroush's view, it is not God who is the author of the Koran. Rather, it is Mohammed. For that reason in his opinion, on the one hand, there are indispensable, eternally valid truths and principles (e.g., God's righteousness or the teaching of life after death); on the other hand, these eternal principles are to be differentiated from temporary directives. Thus, not all statements stand tantamount next to each other. For example, Soroush views following Islamic penal law as temporary and secondary – but his calls to reform the conventional ahistorical approach to revelation and to achieve a contemporary interpretation of Sharia law do not link him to an essentially secular criticism of Islam or Sharia law as such. Instead, Soroush includes religion in a system in which the highest principle is reason. His goal is the establishment of a religious democracy[57] based upon reason, where the individual can put his religion into practice according to his own convictions and not on the basis of coercion and law. In this democracy, which holds human rights in high regard, religion is best protected from any misuse of power and thus it is best cared for. As far as Soroush is concerned, it is reasonable and therefore the guiding principle to adopt human rights and democracy from other non-Islamic states. Reason allows a new interpretation of Islamic sources, because that which is

---

[55] See his personal website http://www.drsoroush.com/index.htm (accessed December 18, 2012).

[56] Mahmoud Sadri and Ahmad Sadri (ed.), *Reason, Freedom, and Democracy in Islam* (Oxford: Oxford University Press, 2000), p. 127.

[57] Compare his remarks on the compatibility of religion and tolerance, ibid., pp. 138ff.

good from the perspective of reason cannot contradict Islam. A necessary goal for Soroush is the establishment of a religiously grounded democracy, thus a democracy in which every citizen can live out his faith but cannot be coerced into a religion by force.[58]

This approach, which differentiates between the eternally revealed word and law of God and the human interpretation and application that is tainted with flaws, has been brought forward by theologians and intellectuals in the past. They have attempted to find an alternative to prevailing textual interpretations without simultaneously sacrificing the eternally valid divine claim of the Koran and Sharia law. If Sharia law tself is not up for discussion, but its interpretation is, the contents of Sharia law are essentially a historical and changeable aggregate – but there would still be a long way to go to justifying equality, civil liberties, and human rights.

---

[58] See details on the life and work of Abdolkarim Soroush on his homepage: http://www.drsoroush.com/English.htm (accessed December 18, 2012).

IV. What are the future prospects for democracy in countries characterized by Islam?

If established theology continues to teach Sharia law as the indispensable law of God in its form as a compendium of commands from the Arabian Peninsula from the time of the seventh to the tenth centuries A.D., and if Mohammed continues to be an inscrutable and timeless role model not only in religious issues but also in his function as a lawgiver and military leader, it will remain difficult for freedom of opinion and political liberties, equal rights for women and men, for Muslims and non-Muslims, a separation of powers, the rule of law, freedom of conscience, and especially freedom of religion to thrive. Democracy does not emerge simply from itself. Indeed, democracy can be supported from without, but it can only be brought into a region in a rather qualified manner. Democracy needs a subsoil in order to grow and thrive. It requires derivation from the philosophical theories within the history of ideas of a culture. Democracy requires a justification based upon worldview foundations of overriding importance which are acknowledged by the majority of the people and are explanatory of democracy. In countries characterized by Islam, in light of what is found to be an overall relatively strong identification with the religion of Islam and the religious values of Islam, there is a key role to be played by Islamic theology in finding a form of reconciliation between classical Islamic theology and human rights, women's rights, and civil liberties (including freedom of religion). This is the case despite all the variety with respect to religious bonds and practice on the part of individuals. Otherwise, over the long term, it will arguably be scarcely possible for stable democratic structures to emerge in the region. The sole example of Turkey is not sufficient as long as, especially in the Arab world, the basic principle of Turkish politics, the separation between the state and religion, is spurned as a model for the future.

If the region is to develop, there is much which is necessary: The creation of many jobs and trainee positions, a functioning educational system, incentives for investment and entrepreneurship, as well as legal security and the guarantee of civil rights and liberties. All of this requires a worldview justification, a philosophical superstructure with which the majority of the population can identify. Those protesting in the Arabellion did not exhibit this philosophical superstructure: They bound themselves in opposition to ubiquitous oppression but were then in disagreement with respect to the concrete configuration of the future, the more so as the dictatorships had not, up to that point, allowed liberal thought and action upon which one could build. However, not only civil rights and liberties are required. Economic development is also urgently needed. Without a just distribution of oil wealth and economic/educational development it will hardly be possible to establish democracies within the region. If there is a further deterioration of living conditions for a broad majority of the population, Islamism can by all means gain ground. Increased civil rights and liberties for the people of this region are urgently desired. However, the essential justification of these civil rights and liberties, the search for a philosophical derivation of these civil rights and liberties, shared by the majority of the people, has not even begun beyond the critically progressive intellectual class.

Literature

Adonis. "Die Sackgasse der Moderne in der arabischen Gesellschaft," in: Erdmute Heller; Hassouna Mosbahi (ed.). *Islam, Demokratie, Moderne. Aktuelle Antworten arabischer Denker.* München: C. H. Beck, 1998, pp. 62-71.

Sarah Albrecht. Islamisches Minderheitenrecht. Yusuf al-Qaradawis Konzept des fiqh al-aqalliyat, Würzburg: Ergon, 2010.

Sami A. Aldeeb Abu-Sahlieh. "Le élit d'Apostasie aujourd'hui et ses Conséquences en Droit Arabe et Musulman," in *Islamochristiania* (20) 1994, pp. 93-116.

Katajun Amirpur. Unterwegs zu einem anderen Islam. Texte iranischer Denker. Freiburg: Herder, 2009.

Allgemeine Erklärung der Menschenrechte im Islam. http://www.way-to-allah.com/dokument/Internationale%20Menschenrechte-Deklaration%20im%20Islam.pdf (Accessed December 18, 2012).

Katajun Amirpur; Ludwig Amman (eds.). Der Islam am Wendepunkt. Liberale und konservative Reformer einer Weltreligion. Freiburg: Herder, 2006.

Ludwig Amman. Cola und Koran. *Das Wagnis einer islamischen Renaissance.* Freiburg: Herder, 2004.

Amnesty International Report 2011. *Zur weltweiten Lage der Menschenrechte.* Frankfurt: S. Fischer, 2011.

Cheryl Benard. Civil Democratic Islam. Partners, Resources, and Strategies. Santa Monica: Rand Corporation, 2003.

Wolfgang Bergsdorf (ed.). Christoph Martin Wieland Vorlesungen: Mohammad M. Shabestari. *Der Islam und die Demokratie.* Erfurt: Sutton Verlag, 2003.

Heiner Bielefeldt. Muslime im säkularen Rechtsstaat. Integrationschancen durch Religionsfreiheit. Bielefeld: Transcript, 2003.

Ernst-Wolfgang Böckenförde: *Staat, Gesellschaft, Freiheit.* Frankfurt: Suhrkamp, 1976.

Katrin Brettfeld; Peter Wetzels. Muslime in Deutschland. Eine Studie des Bundesinnenministeriums zu Integration, Integrationsbarrieren, Religion und Einstellungen zu Demokratie, Rechtsstaat und politisch-religiös motivierter Gewalt. Ergebnisse von Befragungen im Rahmen einer multizentrischen Studie in städtischen Lebensräumen. Hamburg: Universität Hamburg, 2007.

Manfred Brocker; Tine Stein (eds.). *Christentum und Demokratie.* Darmstadt: WGB, 2006.

Wilfried Buchta. "Irans Reformdebatte um Theokratie versus Demokratie," in: Hans Zehetmair (ed.). *Der Islam im Spannungsfeld von Konflikt und Dialog.* Wiesbaden: VS, 2005, pp. 220-235.

"Democracy Index 2011. Democracy under Stress. A Report from the Economist Intelligence Unit," http://www.sida.se/Global/About%20Sida/Så%20arbetar%20vi/EIU_Democracy_Index_Dec2011.pdf (Accessed December 18, 2012).

Demokratie braucht Tugenden. Gemeinsames Wort des Rates der Evangelischen Kirche in Deutschland und der Deutschen Bischofskonferenz zur Zukunft unseres demokratischen Gemeinwesens. Kirchenamt der EKD/Sekretariat der Deutschen Bischofskonferenz: Hannover/Bonn, 2006.

Die Kairoer Erklärung für Menschenrechte im Islam. http://www.dailytalk.ch/wp-content/uploads/Kairoer%20Erklaerung%20der%20OIC.pdf (18.12.2012)

Anne Duncker. Menschenrechte im Islam. Eine Analyse islamischer Erklärungen über die Menschenrechte. Berlin: Wissenschaftlicher Verlag, 2006.

Kevin Dwyer. Arab Voices. The Human Rights Debate in the Middle East. London: Routledge, 1991.

Evangelische Kirche und Freiheitliche Demokratie. Der Staat des Grundgesetzes als Angebot und Aufgabe. Eine Denkschrift der Evangelischen Kirche in Deutschland. Gütersloh: Gütersloher Verlagshaus Gerd Mohn, 1985.

Martin Forstner. "Das Menschenrecht der Religionsfreiheit und des Religionswechsels als Problem der islamischen Staaten," in: *Kanon. Kirche und Staat im Christlichen Osten. Jahrbuch der Gesellschaft für das Recht der Ostkirchen*. Wien: Verlag des Verbandes der wissenschaftlichen Gesellschaften Österreichs, 1991, pp. 105-186.

Freedom in the World 2012. The Arab Uprisings and their Global Repercussions. http://www.freedomhouse.org/sites/default/files/FIW%202012%20Booklet_0.pdf (Accessed 18, 2012).

Theodore Gabriel. *Christian Citizens in an Islamic State. The Pakistan Experience*. Ashgate Aldershot: Publishing Limited, 2007.

Martin Greschat; Jochen-Christoph Kaiser (ed.). *Christentum und Demokratie im 20. Jahrhundert*. Stuttgart: Kohlhammer, 1992.

Armin Hasemann. "Zur Apostasiediskussion im Modernen Ägypten," in: *Die Welt des Islam* 42/1 (2002), pp. 72-121.

Jeffrey Haynes (ed.) Democratization. Special Issue: Religion and Democratizations. 16/6 (2009).

Erdmute Heller; Hassouna Mosbahi (eds.). *Islam, Demokratie, Moderne. Aktuelle Antworten arabischer Denker*. München: C. H. Beck, 1998.

Murad Hofmann. Der Islam im 3. Jahrtausend. Eine Religion im Aufbruch. Kreuzlingen: Diederichs, 2000.

Gerhard Höver. "Grundwerte und Menschenrechte im Islam," in: Bernhard Mensen SVD (ed.). *Grundwerte und Menschenrechte in verschiedenen Kulturen*. Siegburg: Akademie Völker und Kulturen St. Augustin/Steyler Verlag, 1988, pp. 37-51.

William J. Hoye. Demokratie und Christentum. Die christliche Verantwortung für demokratische Prinzipien. Münster: Aschendorff, 1999.

Carsten Jürgensen. Demokratie und Menschenrechte in der arabischen Welt. Positionen arabischer Menschenrechtsaktivisten. Hamburg: Deutsches Orient-Institut, 1994.

Katharina Knüppel. Religionsfreiheit und Apostasie in islamisch geprägten Staaten. Frankfurt: Peter Lang, 2010.

Der Koran. Rudi Paret. Stuttgart: Kohlhammer, 1980[2].

Gudrun Krämer. Gottes Staat als Republik. Reflexionen zeitgenössischer Muslime zu Islam, Menschenrechten und Demokratie. Baden-Baden: Nomos, 1999.

Gudrun Krämer. Demokratie im islam. Der Kampf für Toleranz und Freiheit in der arabischen Welt. München: C. H. Beck, 2011.

Birgit Krawietz. Die Hurma. Schariarechtlicher Schutz vor Eingriffen in die körperliche Unversehrtheit nach arabischen Fatwas des 20. Jahrhunderts. Berlin: Duncker & Humblot, 1991.

Hans Maier. Demokratischer Verfassungsstaat ohne Christentum – Was wäre anders? St. Augustin/Berlin: Konrad-Adenauer-Stiftung, 2006.

Paul Marshall (ed.). Religious Freedom in the World. Lanham: Rowman & Littlefield Publ. Inc., 2008.

Paul Marshall; Nina Shea. Silenced. How Apostasy & Blasphemy Codes are Choking Freedom Worldwide. Oxford: Oxford University Press, 2011.

Sayyid Abul A'la Maududi. Islamic Way of Life. Lahore: Islamic Publications Ltd., 1950/1965[3]/1986.

S. Abu'la Mawdudi. The Islamic Law and Constitution. Lahore: Islamic Publications Ltd., 1955/1980[7].

S. Abul A'la Maududi. Ethical Viewpoint of Islam. Lahore: Islamic Publications Ltd., 1966[2]/1967[3].

Ann Elizabeth Mayer. Islam and Human Rights. Tradition and Politics. Boulder: Westview Press, 1995.

Wolfgang Merkel. "Religion, Fundamentalismus und Demokratie," in: Wolfgang Schluchter (ed.). Fundamentalismus, Terrorismus, Krieg. Weilerswist: Velbrück, 2003.

Thomas Meyer. Was ist Demokratie? Eine diskursive Einführung. Wiesbaden: VS, 2009.

Lorenz Müller. Islam und Menschenrechte. Sunnitische Muslime zwischen Islamismus, Säkularismus und Modernismus. Hamburg: Deutsches Orient-Institut, 1996.

Bahman Nirumand. "Der iranische Reformer Mohsen Kadivar. Anpassung an zeitgemäße Lesarten des Islam." http://de.qantara.de/Anpassung-an-zeitgemaesse-Lesarten-des-Islam/849c812i1p97/ (December 18, 2012).

Yusuf al-Qaradawi. al-halal wa-'l-haram fi 'l-islam. Dar ihya' al-kutub al-arabiya: Kairo, 1960

Jusuf al-Qaradawi. Erlaubtes und Verbotenes im Islam. München: SKD Bavaria, 1989.

Yusuf al-Qaradawi. fi fiqh al-aqalliyat al-muslima. hayat al-muslimin wasat al-mujtama'at al-uhra, Kairo: Dar ash-shuruq, 2001.

Anton Rauscher (ed.). *Die fragile Demokratie - The Fragility of Democracy.* Berlin: Duncker & Humblot, 2007.

Mahmoud Sadri; Ahmad Sadri (eds.). *Reason, Freedom, and Democracy in Islam.* Oxford: Oxford University Press, 2000.

Thomas Schirrmacher. "Demokratie und christliche Ethik," in: *Aus Politik und Zeitgeschichte* 14/2009. http://www.bpb.de/apuz/32086/demokratie-und-christliche-ethik?p=all (December 18, 2012).

Thomas Schirrmacher. *Menschenrechte. Anspruch und Wirklichkeit.* Holzgerlingen:SCM Hännsler, 2012.

Manfred G. Schmidt. *Demokratietheorien. Eine Einführung.* VS: Wiesbaden 2008/4.

Ursi Schweizer. *Muslime in Europa.* Staatsbürgerschaft und Islam in einer liberalen und säkularen Demokratie. Berlin: Klaus Schwarz, 2008.

Roman Seidel. "Porträt Shabestari. Glaube, Freiheit und Vernunft," Qantara: December 1, 2004, http://de.qantara.de/Glaube-Freiheit-und-Vernunft/3240c3334i1p396/ (November 5, 2012).

Mohammad Mojtahed Shabestari. "Demokratie und Religiosität," in: Katajun Amirpur. *Unterwegs zu einem anderen Islam. Texte iranischer Denker.* Freiburg: Herder, 2009, pp. 25-36.

Shahid Shaykh Sayyid Qutb. *Ma'alim fi t-tariq. Zeichen auf dem Weg.* Köln: Al-Azr/M. Rassoul, 2005.

Ali Abdallah Siddiq. "Human Rights in Islam," in: *The Muslim World League Journal,* Vol. 25, No. 8, December 1997, pp. 35-39.

Hannes Stein. Moses und die Offenbarung der Demokratie. Berlin: Rowohlt, 1998.

Mahmoud Mohamed Taha. *The Second Message of Islam.* Translation and Introduction by Abdullahi Ahmed an-Na'im. Syracuse: Syracuse University Press, 1987.

Bassam Tibi. Im Schatten Allahs. Der Islam und die Menchenrechte. München: Piper, 1996.

Gereon Vogel. Blasphemie. Die Affäre Rushdie in religionswissenschaftlicher Sicht. Zugleich ein Beitrag zum Begriff der Religion. Frankfurt: Peter Lang, 1997.

Thomas Zimmermanns. *Demokratie aus christlicher Sicht.* Bonn: VKW, 2008.

World Evangelical Alliance

World Evangelical Alliance is a global ministry working with local churches around the world to join in common concern to live and proclaim the Good News of Jesus in their communities. WEA is a network of churches in 129 nations that have each formed an evangelical alliance and over 100 international organizations joining together to give a worldwide identity, voice and platform to more than 600 million evangelical Christians. Seeking holiness, justice and renewal at every level of society – individual, family, community and culture, God is glorified and the nations of the earth are forever transformed.

Christians from ten countries met in London in 1846 for the purpose of launching, in their own words, "a new thing in church history, a definite organization for the expression of unity amongst Christian individuals belonging to different churches." This was the beginning of a vision that was fulfilled in 1951 when believers from 21 countries officially formed the World Evangelical Fellowship. Today, 150 years after the London gathering, WEA is a dynamic global structure for unity and action that embraces 600 million evangelicals in 129 countries. It is a unity based on the historic Christian faith expressed in the evangelical tradition. And it looks to the future with vision to accomplish God's purposes in discipling the nations for Jesus Christ.

Commissions:

- Theology
- Missions
- Religious Liberty
- Women's Concerns
- Youth
- Information Technology

Initiatives and Activities

- Ambassador for Human Rights
- Ambassador for Refugees
- Creation Care Task Force
- Global Generosity Network
- International Institute for Religious Freedom
- International Institute for Islamic Studies
- Leadership Institute
- Micah Challenge
- Global Human Trafficking Task Force
- Peace and Reconciliation Initiative
- UN-Team

Church Street Station
P.O. Box 3402
New York, NY 10008-3402
Phone +[1] 212 233 3046
Fax +[1] 646-957-9218
www.worldea.org

Giving Hands

GIVING HANDS GERMANY (GH) was established in 1995 and is officially recognized as a nonprofit foreign aid organization. It is an international operating charity that – up to now – has been supporting projects in about 40 countries on four continents. In particular we care for orphans and street children. Our major focus is on Africa and Central America. GIVING HANDS always mainly provides assistance for self-help and furthers human rights thinking.

The charity itself is not bound to any church, but on the spot we are co-operating with churches of all denominations. Naturally we also cooperate with other charities as well as governmental organizations to provide assistance as effective as possible under the given circumstances.

The work of GIVING HANDS GERMANY is controlled by a supervisory board. Members of this board are Manfred Feldmann, Colonel V. Doner and Kathleen McCall. Dr. Christine Schirrmacher is registered as legal manager of GIVING HANDS at the local district court. The local office and work of the charity are coordinated by Rev. Horst J. Kreie as executive manager. Dr. theol. Thomas Schirrmacher serves as a special consultant for all projects.

Thanks to our international contacts companies and organizations from many countries time and again provide containers with gifts in kind which we send to the different destinations where these goods help to satisfy elementary needs. This statutory purpose is put into practice by granting nutrition, clothing, education, construction and maintenance of training centers at home and abroad, construction of wells and operation of water treatment systems, guidance for self-help and transportation of goods and gifts to areas and countries where needy people live.

GIVING HANDS has a publishing arm under the leadership of Titus Vogt, that publishes human rights and other books in English, Spanish, Swahili and other languages.

These aims are aspired to the glory of the Lord according to the basic Christian principles put down in the Holy Bible.

Baumschulallee 3a • D-53115 Bonn • Germany
Phone: +49 / 228 / 695531 • Fax +49 / 228 / 695532
www.gebende-haende.de • info@gebende-haende.de

International Institute for Religious Freedom

Purpose and Aim

The "International Institute for Religious Freedom" (IIRF) is a network of professors, researchers, academics, specialists and university institutions from all continents with the aim of working towards:

- The establishment of reliable facts on the restriction of religious freedom worldwide.
- The making available of results of such research to other researchers, politicians, advocates, as well as the media.
- The introduction of the subject of religious freedom into academic research and curricula.
- The backing up of advocacy for victims of violations of religious freedom in the religious, legal and political world.
- Serving discriminated and persecuted believers and academics wherever they are located. Publications and other research will be made available as economically and as readily available as possible to be affordable in the Global South.

Tools

The IIRF encourages all activities that contribute to the understanding of religious freedom. These include:

- Dissemination of existing literature, information about archives, compilation of bibliographies etc.
- Production and dissemination of new papers, journals and books.
- Gathering and analysis of statistics and evidence.
- Supplying of ideas and materials to universities and institutions of theological education to encourage the inclusion of religious freedom issues into curricula.
- Guiding postgraduate students in research projects either personally or in cooperation with the universities and educational institutions.
- Representation at key events where opportunity is given to strengthen connections with the wider religious liberty community and with politicians, diplomats and media.

Online / Contact:

- www.iirf.eu / info@iirf.eu

Institute of Islamic Studies

The protestant "Institute of Islamic Studies" is a network of scholars in Islamic studies and is carried out by the Evangelical Alliance in Germany, Austria and Switzerland.

Churches, the political arena, and society at large are provided foundational information relating to the topic of 'Islam' through research and the presentation thereof via publications, adult education seminars, and democratic political discourse.

Research Focus

As far as our work is concerned, the focus is primarily on Islam in Europe, the global development of Islamic theology and of Islamic fundamentalism, as well as a respectful and issue-related meeting of Christians and Muslims. In the process, misunderstandings about Islam and Muslims can be cleared up, and problematic developments in Islamic fundamentalism and political Islam are explained. Through our work we want to contribute to engaging Muslims in an informed and fair manner.

What we do

Lectures, seminars, and conferences for public authorities, churches, political audiences, and society at large

- Participation in special conferences on the topic of Islam
- The publication of books in German, English, and Spanish
- The preparation of scholarly studies for the general public
- Special publications on current topics
- Production of a German-English journal entitled "Islam and Christianity"
- Regular press releases with commentaries on current events from a scholarly Islamic studies perspective
- Academic surveys and experts' reports for advisory boards of government
- Regular news provided as summaries of Turkish and Arab language internet publications
- Fatwa archive
- Website with a collection of articles

Islam and Christianity

Journal of the Institute of Islamic Studies
and the International Institute of Islamic Studies

- German/English. All articles in both languages

- Topics of current issues: Women in Islam, Human Rights in Islam, Sharia law, Shii Islam.

- Editor: Prof. Dr. Christine Schirrmacher
  Executive Editor: Carsten Polanz

- ISSN 1616-8917

- 48 pp. twice annually

- 9,20 € per year including postage (airmail on request)

- **Sample copies and subscription**:
  IfI · Pf 7427 · D-53074 Bonn · Germany
  info@islaminstitut.de

- **Download** under www.islaminstitut.de/zeitschrift.20.0.html

ISLAM UND CHRISTLICHER GLAUBE
ISLAM AND CHRISTIANITY

Zeitschrift des
Instituts für Islamfragen (IfI)
Journal of the
Institute of Islamic Studies
ISSN 1616-8917

Nr. 1/2005 (5. Jg.)

Inhalt/Contents

/VTR

Institute for Islamic Studies (IfI)
of the Evangelical Alliance in Germany, Austria, Switzerland

International Institute of Islamic Studies (IIIS)
of the World Evangelical Alliance

IfI · Pf 7427 · D-53074 Bonn · Germany · info@islaminstitut.de

www.islaminstitute.net

International Institute
of Islamic Studies

Martin Bucer Seminary

Faithful to biblical truth
Cooperating with the Evangelical Alliance
Reformed

Solid training for the Kingdom of God

- Alternative theological education
- Study while serving a church or working another job
- Enables students to remain in their own churches
- Encourages independent thinking
- Learning from the growth of the universal church.

Academic

- For the Bachelor's degree: 180 Bologna-Credits
- For the Master's degree: 120 additional Credits
- Both old and new teaching methods: All day seminars, independent study, term papers, etc.

Our Orientation:

- Complete trust in the reliability of the Bible
- Building on reformation theology
- Based on the confession of the German Evangelical Alliance
- Open for innovations in the Kingdom of God

Our Emphasis:

- The Bible
- Ethics and Basic Theology
- Missions
- The Church

Our Style:

- Innovative
- Relevant to society
- International
- Research oriented
- Interdisciplinary

Structure

- 15 study centers in 7 countries with local partners
- 5 research institutes
- President: Prof. Dr. Thomas Schirrmacher
  Vice President: Prof. Dr. Thomas K. Johnson
- Deans: Thomas Kinker, Th.D.;
  Titus Vogt, lic. theol., Carsten Friedrich, M.Th.

Missions through research

- Institute for Religious Freedom
- Institute for Islamic Studies
- Institute for Life and Family Studies
- Institute for Crisis, Dying, and Grief Counseling
- Institute for Pastoral Care

www.bucer.eu • info@bucer.eu
Berlin I Bielefeld I Bonn I Chemnitz I Hamburg I Munich I Pforzheim
Innsbruck I Istanbul I Izmir I Linz I Prague I São Paulo I Tirana I Zurich